Get Set for Communication Studies

Get Set for Communication Studies

Will Barton and Andrew Beck

Edinburgh University Press

Edinburgh University Press Ltd
22 George Square, Edinburgh

Typeset in Sabon
by Servis Filmsetting Ltd, Manchester, and
printed and bound in Finland by
WS Bookwell

A CIP record for this book is available from the British Library

ISBN 0 7486 2029 X (paperback)

CONTENTS

ACKNOWLEDGEMENTS

A book is never produced just by the people whose names appear on the cover. So we need to thank those people who have helped us with this project.

Sarah Edwards of Edinburgh University Press gave us the green light for this project and has been the very spirit of kindness and understanding in ensuring we brought it to completion.

Our colleague John Lister conducted the on-line interviews with graduates of Coventry University's Communication Culture and Media undergraduate degree programme which appear in chapter 3.

The Coventry graduates, busy professionals all, were kind enough to find time to tell us about their exciting and demanding lives in communication and media industries.

Students in Coventry, London, Newcastle-under-Lyme and Stratford-upon-Avon have been on the receiving end of our efforts to teach Communication Studies for more years than we care to remember. We hope that age has improved us and that we now manage to say what we want to say more clearly and more succinctly than we did when we started out.

Tony and Pat Leahy created a delightful and convivial environment where at least half of this book was written.

Mikesh Chauhan produced the graphics for the section on Visual and Graphic Communication.

Thank you all.
W.B. and A.B.

LIST OF ILLUSTRATIONS

INTRODUCTION

This book is the latest in a series of titles intended to be read by students who are about to start undergraduate studies at UK universities when they haven't taken the subject as part of their 16–19 education. With some subjects the gap between school sixth form or college education and university undergraduate education isn't that big. Either you will have studied the subject in your last years at school or college, or you will find that the university curriculum represents a clear continuation of the 'A' level or AVCE or GNVQ or Highers or Baccalaureate curriculum. Of course, all university tutors prefer to insist that there is little resemblance between what school and college teachers do and what they, as university lecturers, do, but in reality we feel they protest too much.

We accept that there are differences of emphasis and, in general, UK undergraduate courses in the arts, humanities and social sciences will expose students to more critical theory and more critical thinking than they have previously been used to. But Communication Studies is something of an exception. First, there is no GCSE Communication Studies specification available to be studied by any student anywhere in the UK. Secondly, there is an 'A' level Communication Studies specification but, while there is significant take-up of this specification at AS level barely half of the students who sit the AS go on to take the second set of three modules to gain them the full 'A' level award. Thirdly, Communication Studies is now frequently taken as part of a cross-disciplinary or interdisciplinary programme drawing on elements of Cultural Studies (which is not available as a GCSE or an 'A' level at all) and on vocational Media Studies programmes (where the media industries emphasised at school or college tend to be narrower than at university). Thus, the vast majority of students who apply, and are accepted, for a place on a Communication Studies programme or a Communication Studies-based programme tend to have had no previous formal experience of studying Communication before they arrive at university. So, while most, if not all, students who follow undergraduate programmes in English, Media Studies or Psychology will feel they have a clear picture of the breadth and range of their subjects and that they already possess many of the critical, analytical and evaluative tools used to work with their subject, this is rarely the case with Communication Studies students.

It's for that reason that this book has been written. We believe that it can be easily read in bite-sized pieces over the long vacation between school or college and university. And we hope that it isn't a difficult read despite the fact that for most readers much of what is offered here will be new. But in case you feel we are unnecessarily emphasising the size of the gap between what you have studied at school or college and what you will study on a Communication Studies programme at a UK university let's put your mind at rest a little. Most students following arts, humanities or social science programmes at UK universities will experience a similar disorientation when they begin their undergraduate studies. Despite the fact that a student has, for example, successfully completed an 'A' level English Literature programme, when they arrive at university to take a programme with the same name they are frequently confronted with something they barely recognise at all. In *Doing English* Robert Eaglestone writes about the gap that exists between what students experience when studying English at 'A' level, International Baccalaureate and Access programmes, and what they experience when they go to university to study English. He offers a useful picture to help explain this gap

if you had gone into a large bookshop twenty years ago, you would have found shelves and shelves of novels, poems and plays. You would also have found a section called 'literary criticism', which had studies on writers and their work. But today if you go into a big enough bookshop, you will also find a section called 'literary theory', which simply wouldn't have been there twenty years ago. This 'literary theory' section – containing books on feminism and postmodernism and all sorts of other subjects – might not seem to reflect the English taught in schools and colleges at all. However, the books in the 'literary theory' section are about new ways of doing English that have been taken up and used in higher education. (Eaglestone 2000: 2)

So you, as an intending Communication Studies student, won't be alone. Indeed, by scanning the Contents page of this book you might have already spotted that when doing Communication Studies at university you'll be using some of the same tools that you would if you were doing English. And some of you might be following programmes that combine elements of English and Communication Studies.

HOW THIS BOOK IS ORGANISED

Having set the scene for both the writing and the reading of this book we now need to explain how the book is organised.

It's divided into two parts and both Parts I and II are divided into six chapters. Broadly speaking, Part I is about the subject of Communication Studies, and Part II is about the skills you'll need to follow a Communication Studies programme effectively. Of course, such a division isn't one that Communication Studies academics either embrace or approve of – at its best we believe that Communication Studies represents a synthesis of studies and skills, of theory and practice. But a book does have to have an organising principle. So Part I will address the questions: Where did Communication Studies come from? What is Communication Studies? What do Communication Studies programmes in UK universities look like? What are the broad areas of study within Communication Studies programmes? And, how do I go about doing Communication Studies? While Part II will address the very practical questions of how I go about preparing myself for effective work as a Communication Studies undergraduate.

In Part I we explain where Communication Studies came from in a UK context. Communication Studies has a longer and older history in, for example, US higher education, but we will not explore the US experience as this book is intended for students about to join a UK Communication Studies undergraduate programme. We then move on to look at what is actually meant by Communication Studies. As with many subjects in higher education in the UK this is not an easy question to address or answer. Indeed, the prime characterising feature of many undergraduate programmes in UK universities is their questioning of the very subject itself; nothing is taken for granted and all aspects of the subject, including attempts to write its history, will be questioned. (At the very least Communication Studies has many histories rather than one.) Then we move on to give a brief overview of what you might expect to study when you enrol for a Communication Studies programme at a UK university. As with the previous chapter this won't necessarily be a clear and unambiguous matter. The sheer range of programmes available under the umbrella of Communication Studies is staggering. What's more amazing is the number of routes through those programmes: many Communication Studies programmes are constructed on a modular basis where students have a large degree of choice over which modules they take and which they don't. In this way students can approach the modular structure like a cafeteria from which they can build a meal of their own choice, often quite unlike the programmes of other students alongside whom they're studying. In chapter 4 we offer a map of the field and briefly outline ten aspects of Communication Studies. When you arrive at university you'll recognise that some of these areas are the actual titles of modules, or routes (or pathways), through undergraduate programmes, or the programme titles themselves – for example, Mass Communication. This map isn't extensive or exclusive, but it is a map for beginners. Using Jean Baudrillard's phrase, though not exactly as he intended it (but who indeed does from a postmodern perspective?), 'The map precedes the territory'. You'll probably find the fifth chapter of Part I the most useful one in your early days of undergraduate Communication Studies. It's what we call the Communication Studies Toolkit: you'll be introduced to ten key perspectives from and through which you can do Communication Studies. You might have encountered some of these before, if only by name. You will also recognise that two of them – feminism and postmodernism – are perspectives that Robert Eaglestone identified as part of the toolkit students have to acquire to do English in UK higher education. We'd argue that they are essential tools for making sense of the world in which we live, irrespective of whether you're a Communication Studies undergraduate or not. The sixth and final chapter of Part I offers you some further reading. Unlike many other books that are intended as primers but which direct their readers to long lists of further reading we have tried to restrict ourselves in how much further or additional reading we point you to. We have been guided by the notion of how much time we feel you could reasonably devote to reading about and around Communication Studies in the period you have between school or college and university, bearing in mind that there'll be lots of other things you'll want or need to do in this time. In the Communication Studies Toolkit we offer you some very precise and concise additional readings you can undertake to consolidate your learning. These are rarely whole books; more often they are small sections or chapters of books or parts of websites. With our Further Reading chapter we offer you only three further texts: one is a textbook, the second is an anthology of key readings and the third is a website. We offer you a very focused tour of those parts of these texts which will further reinforce and consolidate your learning about Communication Studies.

In Part II we explore the skills necessary to do Communication Studies. Much of the advice offered is of a generic character and as such can be applied to many arts, humanities and social science programmes in UK higher education. First of all we offer advice about effective studying, with particular attention being paid to how you can read more efficiently. This might seem unnecessary or condescending, but it isn't intended to be. To be an effective student you need to be smart about how you read. That means being more selective, more focused and more economic in terms of what and how you read. Next we offer you advice about how you can effectively manage your time at university. Again, this might seem like common sense and something everybody is born with, but it's not. It's perfectly possible to devote a phenomenal amount of time to studying and not be an effective student. (Your work won't be assessed by how much time you've devoted to it; it'll be assessed on what it says and how it says it.) Next we look at how you can make effective use of the time you have for tutorials. Our advice here is particularly geared towards students taking undergraduate Communication Studies programmes in the new or modern universities where student numbers are usually quite large and where access to teaching staff is limited. We use some case studies here to flesh out how you can go about preparing for tutorials and how you can consolidate the use of the time you have to share with teaching staff. Next we look at some ways in which you can be an effective student in lectures. Then we examine how those skills acquired and practised when reading, when having tutorials and when listening in lectures can all be combined when researching, planning, writing and revising essays on undergraduate Communication Studies programmes. Here again we adopt a case study approach. Finally, we offer you some advice about how to prepare effectively for examinations and how to sit them.

A NOTE ABOUT REFERENCING

When you wrote extended essays or assignments at school or college you might have been asked to provide a bibliography at the end of the piece of work. Your teachers might have introduced you to a specific system for presenting the works you had consulted. When you begin life as an undergraduate student of Communication Studies one of the first things you will be introduced to is a system for referencing. This covers not only how you present details of the works you have consulted when writing your essay, but also how you make concise and unobtrusive reference to those works within the body of your essay itself. There are any number of systems used in UK universities. No one system is any better than any other; every university department will have its own preference. What is important is that you understand how those referencing systems work. And it's vital you put that understanding into practice as soon as you start submitting written work at university.

Many UK university Communication Studies departments use the Harvard referencing system. When we quoted from Robert Eaglestone's *Doing English* earlier we used the Harvard system to acknowledge that we were making a quotation and to specify the page in the work from which we were quoting. The way in which the Harvard system works is this. All works consulted or quoted are presented in full in the bibliography which appears at the end of the essay. Details are presented in this sequence: the author's family name followed by a comma followed by the initial letter(s) of their first name(s) followed by the year of publication in parenthesis followed by the full title of the work in italics followed by a comma followed by the place of publication followed by a colon followed by the publisher's name followed by a full stop. If you consulted this book in researching and writing an essay this is how you would present the details in your bibliography:

Barton, W. and Beck, A. (2005) *Get Set for Communication Studies*, Edinburgh: Edinburgh University Press.

And if you wanted to acknowledge that you had consulted Eaglestone this is how you would reference his work:

Eaglestone, R. (2000) *Doing English*, London: Routledge.

You would also use the Harvard system to refer to works consulted within the body of your essay. This is part and parcel of being an effective scholar. Nowadays any tutor would question any unreferenced quotation in an essay; they would assume this came either from sloppy scholarship or an over-fertile imagination. If you have done the reading and are quoting accurately, then you will be expected to provide a precise reference to where you got the quotation from. But to quote all the details of the work consulted in full within the body of the essay would be intrusive and clumsy and would unduly interfere with the effective reading of the essay. So the Harvard system has a succinct way of providing this reference. This is how it works. After you have presented the quotation you open a parenthesis, write the family name of the author, then you write the year of publication, then a colon, then the page (or pages) where the quotation is taken from; finally you close the parenthesis. That's the system we used when we quoted from Robert Eaglestone's book *Doing English* earlier in this Introduction:

(Eaglestone 2000: 2)

Anyone reading this would find that their reading wasn't interrupted by this brief reference and they would know that if they wanted the full details of the work being referenced, they should go to the bibliography at the end of the essay. For the present they would know that the author being quoted has the family name Eaglestone, they would know that the author published the book in 2000, and they would know that the page where the quotation is taken from was page 2.

In this book where we point you to further or additional reading we've used a simple referencing system – pretty much like one you've previously used in your studies. This will give you sufficient details as you'll need to get the books from your school or college library or local public library or bookstore, but when you begin your undergraduate studies you will be expected to use a referencing system. So in the bibliography at the end of this book we present all the books we refer you to in this book using the Harvard referencing system.

And now over to you.

We hope you enjoy reading this book. We really hope that you can read it before you go up to university (but we have a sneaky suspicion that you might want to refer to it in the early days of your undergraduate studies). We trust that it will prepare you for your undergraduate Communication Studies programme. We believe that Communication Studies is one of the most exciting and most demanding subjects you can do at university. We want the reading of this book to be your passport to the wonders of the world of Communication Studies.

Will Barton and Andrew Beck
Coventry and Leamington Spa, March 2005

PART I
WHAT IS COMMUNICATION STUDIES?

1 COMMUNICATION STUDIES IN THE UK

This chapter offers a history of Communication Studies in the UK in both further and higher education. It will provide you with an historical backdrop to the study of Communication. It will also give you something of an explanation about why Communication Studies sometimes seems hard to pin down as a subject: its interdisciplinary character proves liberating to some people and distinctly confusing and frustrating to others.

The story of Communication Studies in further and higher education in the UK is also very much the story of post-16 education in the UK in the past forty years. Many of the innovations and changes in the post-16 curriculum – the substitution of coursework for examinations; the introduction of new, more modern subjects; the modularisation of programmes; the encouraging of greater independence of students in their learning – all happened in Communication Studies and frequently happened first in Communication Studies. Further, the story of Communication Studies is set against the backdrop of some of the most challenging ideas to enter UK education. In addition, for many people who have been involved in teaching and researching Communication Studies for nearly forty years, the story has also been about a progressive move to look outside of and beyond acutely British attitudes and perspectives – initially by looking to Europe, and latterly to the whole world. Finally, the story of Communication Studies runs in parallel to changes in the status and the work of institutions in post-war UK education: for example, the expansion of arts, humanities and social science programmes in further education colleges, the emergence of polytechnics, and the collapsing of the distinction between polytechnics and universities.

Where did the story start? It's difficult to offer a definitive version (one of the many fascinating features of Communication Studies is the way in which it offers many different, often divergent, and sometimes conflicting, stories about not only how it came into being but also about what it actually is), but some features of its history (or histories) are indisputable. What we are going to do here is to rehearse the development of Communication Studies in UK further and higher education from the late 1950s to the present day. Although these two narratives intersect and have influenced each other, we will deal with them separately: first, the story in further education, and secondly, the story in higher education.

In the Introduction to this book we said that we would concern ourselves only with Communication Studies in an educational context in the UK, but a few words about Communication Studies outside the UK in the immediate post-war years may help contextualise what follows.

There is a longer history of the study of communication in the United States. One of the key theorisations of and about communication was that first published by the American mathematician and information theorist Claude E. Shannon in 1948. By the 1950s and 1960s large numbers of US students were taking whole degree programmes with titles such as Communication Arts. Moreover, students were able to take courses (or modules) in Communication as part of wider arts, humanities or business and management degrees. Bob Dylan, in a 1963 pen-portrait of his life to that point in time, reported that he took 'communication class' at the University of Minnesota (Dylan in Hedin 2004: 4). Those degree courses often had a very strong vocational orientation, being designed from the perspective that Communication could be taught with the precision and exactitude of hard science. Thus it is likely that the 'communication class' that Dylan took (or in his case didn't take) was not designed to prepare him for a career as a songwriter and recording artist but rather was designed to form part of a general education as formulated by post-war US educationalists. But educationalists in the US were astute in identifying the expansion of work opportunities in what we would now routinely refer to as the communication, cultural, information and media industries. And they were similarly astute in taking steps to ensure that appropriate training programmes were available for students wishing to work in communication-based industries. One simple example would be the long history of Journalism Schools in US universities. Any student taking 'A' level Communication Studies between 1976 and 2000 or any student following a BA Communication Studies programme between 1976 and the mid- to late 1980s would have been taking courses that bore a significant resemblance to those post-war US courses in communication.

In mainland Europe there is a long tradition of students being educated within a philosophical and conceptual framework which corresponds to what were perceived as new initiatives in Communication Studies (and English, Film Studies, Media Studies, Sociology and Philosophy) from the 1970s onwards in the UK. In France the pole position of Philosophy in the high school curriculum has long since meant that French students work using concepts and intellectual methods that only a very small number of UK students do (the very small number of students who take 'A' level Philosophy or the relatively small number of students who study Philosophy as undergraduates). In addition, students in European countries such as France, Italy, Spain and Sweden are routinely taught about key moments and key phases in European intellectual histories and movements which UK students never encounter until they enter higher education – and then only on certain programmes such as Communication Studies.

It is difficult to be precise about when Communication was first taught in the UK, but it is possible to trace various histories of the appearances of it in education. In post-war further education the predominant vehicle for delivery of training was the technical college. UK educationalists determined that technical colleges would be the main provider of vocational training for people working in occupational sectors ranging from heavy industry, such as engineering and mining, to white-collar professional sectors, such as business and commerce. The majority of students following these programmes attended technical college one day a week on what was called 'day release'. The government's education ministers and advisers felt that these students should receive a rounded education. To that end, White Papers published in 1959 and 1962 recommended that there should be a General Studies and/or Liberal Studies component in these education and training programmes. So from that time until 1978 all students on day release training programmes spent one hour a week being taught General or Liberal Studies (though the terminology wasn't that precise and it was often difficult to differentiate between one technical college's General Studies and another technical college's Liberal Studies).

For a short while these General or Liberal Studies classes were taught by the teachers that delivered the main occupational-related classes, but very soon teachers were recruited (and eventually trained) to be General and Liberal Studies specialists. From a contemporary perspective it's easy to be quite cynical about the form these classes took, but in one incarnation they consisted of young, liberal-minded teachers exhorting quite conservative students to be critical about the editorial pieces of right-wing UK newspapers, or to appreciate traditionally elite art forms such as theatre and opera. Tom Sharpe's 1976 novel *Wilt* features such a Liberal Studies teacher the bane of whose working life is Meat One (most classes in technical colleges had titles of brutal simplicity, being categorised as they were by their occupation and their year of study: Engineering 1, Craft and Fabrication 2, Welding 3, Catering 4, Mining 5, and so on). Early on in *Wilt* the novel's hero memorably attempts to teach Meat One about the problematic character of human beings using William Golding's *Lord of the Flies* as his text, but they are in no condition to respond to his liberal-humanist overtures as they have arrived at the class as they always do – late and drunk. To add to the misery of many committed General and Liberal Studies teachers the classes had no formal examinations: all the craft and technician students did was attend the classes (or not) and participate in the classes (or not). Many students could not see the point of these studies and regarded them as an imposition. Indeed, many of the teachers who taught the vocational, examined classes failed to see the point of the General and Liberal Studies classes as well. As a result the classes were often timetabled at the beginning or the end of very long college days; this proved a further disincentive to teachers and students alike.

During the 1970s radical changes in the economy and in government economic policies meant that the number of people working in heavy industry declined dramatically in the UK. Apart from the fact that job opportunities in heavy manufacturing and production industries were getting more and more scarce increasing numbers of young people didn't want to follow their parents into blue-collar work but rather had ambitions to work in white-collar industries and professions. For many of these occupations young people didn't obtain work and then get sponsored by their employer to attend college on a day release basis; rather, they had to obtain relevant qualifications before they began work. Thus the 1970s witnessed a huge expansion in the numbers of students attending college on a full-time basis. (Many colleges began to characterise themselves more and more as further education colleges. This signalled the changing character of their work and the occupations they were preparing young people for; many young people were no longer being prepared for jobs that could in any way be classified as technical.)

Many of the students who entered further education colleges in the 1970s wanted to maximise the work or educational opportunities available to them after college and so chose to study 'A' level programmes rather than unified business, clerical or secretarial courses. Many students were attracted to taking 'A' levels at further education colleges not only because of the (then) distinctly different atmosphere of the colleges, but also because of the wider range of 'A' level subjects offered. While many schools were slow to offer 'A' levels in subjects such as Economics, Law, Psychology, Sociology or Theatre Studies, further education colleges were quick to seize the opportunity to do just that. And many of these new 'A' level subjects were taught by teachers who came from families with no tradition whatsoever of working in the professions generally or in education specifically.

Many of those further education college teachers were themselves part of the previous decade's social and educational revolution. For most of the twentieth century higher education in the UK has been the preserve of a social elite. None of the massive historical upheavals of the twentieth century seem to have changed this situation. At the end of the Second World War the US government passed the G.I. Bill, which guaranteed free access to higher education to all service personnel returning from active service; there was no such parallel positive move in the UK. But the Conservative government did create a number of new universities, which first opened their doors to students in 1965. These universities boasted new buildings, were built on greenfield sites just outside major towns and cities, attracted many young lecturers, and seized the opportunity to teach new subjects in the arts, humanities, social sciences, and new sciences and technologies. In addition, a significant number of students who attended these universities came from families where children traditionally had not gone to university. Graduates in the newly emboldened disciplines such as Economics or Sociology thus found themselves in the vanguard of a movement which stood to have significant impact on UK education and society.

Upon graduating many of these young people joined the teaching profession – in the new universities or the further education colleges – working to broaden and soften the curriculum of those institutions. Most of the teachers who began to deliver Communication Studies courses from the late 1970s onwards did not have formal qualifications in Communication Studies (because the programmes hadn't existed when they were undergraduates), but they were ideally suited to work in the discipline by virtue of their social, economic, educational and family backgrounds: they were a newly enfranchised class of teachers who positively embraced a theoretically rigorous, forward-looking discipline that was about Now rather than Then. (This is why it would be a mistake to think that the introduction of Communication as a subject into further and higher education came from simple compliance with government directive: on the contrary, much pioneering work in Communication Studies in education in the UK happened because activist teachers made it happen.)

General and Liberal Studies as a non-examined component of technician education all but disappeared in 1978. This was the year that the government-formed bodies the BEC (the Business Education Council) and TEC (the Technician Education Council) became the large organisations overseeing the majority of vocational education courses in UK colleges. These two bodies had been formed two years earlier and were intended to replace the large number of regional bodies that had until then designed and awarded qualifications for students in technical colleges. All of the courses offered by BEC and TEC had modules which were very much the successors of General and Liberal Studies, and those modules were usually taught by the staff who had previously taught General and Liberal Studies classes. In Business Studies programmes the modules were called People and Communication and in Technician Studies programmes the modules were called General and Communication Studies. The modules were designed as part of integrated, vocationally oriented programmes delivered by integrated teams of teachers – and they were assessed. Accordingly, not only was Communication's status as a subject raised but also the status and esteem of the teachers who delivered it was similarly enhanced. But this status rise was not without its negativeside: the conception of Communication in these programmes was an acutely vocational one – communication was all about oiling the wheels of commerce and industry, it was about making the existing system work better; it was not about critically examining it and proposing alternatives. It is probably from these days that the critical distinction in education between Communication Skills and Communication Studies dates. Communication in the new BEC and TEC courses was thought of as a skill necessary to effective and efficient work; it was not thought of as a critical tool with which to analyse social processes. It's the skills concept of Communication that has been passed on and developed in vocational training from those days to the present. And that vocational concept of Communication has been extended to areas of general education such as the National Curriculum. From the 1970s to the present day Communication has been a key element in a diverse range of educational programmes and qualifications. City and Guilds (CCGLI) developed qualifications in Communication Skills; BEC and TEC (which became BTEC and then Edexcel) introduced the notion of core (subsequently key) skills, one of which was Communication; and young people in secondary education were formally assessed and certificated in three key skills, one of which was Communication. This is why, when educationalists talk about Communication, they are frequently referring to two distinctly different notions: Communication as a general skill (Communication Skills) and Communication as an object and means of analysis (Communication Studies).

But the Communication Studies approach was not abandoned in the 1970s. Rather, its position was strengthened. As part of a greater initiative to develop newer, more modern 'A' levels in the 1970s the Associated Examining Board (AEB, now part of AQA) published the syllabus for its 'A' level Communication Studies. The syllabus first became available to students in 1976 and those students sat the first 'A' Level Communication Studies examinations in 1978. One of the stated aims of the original AEB syllabus was that it was designed:

> To investigate the use and appropriateness of the various means of communication in such fields of human activity as family life, immediate social groups, commerce, industry, politics, education, entertainment and the arts.

This quite clearly reflected the progressive motivation of those teachers who had attended the new universities in the late 1960s and early 1970s taking arts, humanities and social science courses. As part of a School Council project investigating the role of English in the 16–19 curriculum John Dixon led a team which published a report on their findings in 1979. The team studied those first groups of students taking 'A' level Communication Studies. They published some of the statements those students made about their motivation for taking the 'A' level:

'It seems it will be useful to help communicate with people and understand society.'

'Communication is about all of us and therefore the understanding of it will be beneficial to each of us in our role in society.'

'I'm personally very interested in the way people communicate, often without realising they are doing so.'

(Dixon 1979: 73)

The 'A' level had four components, or papers, as follows:

Paper 1 – a traditional examination paper divided into four sections: Means of Communication; Theories of Communication, Mass Communications; and Development of Communications. Students were required to write four essays, one from each section, in three hours in the examination room. Paper 1 had a 30 per cent weighting or value.

Paper 2 – a case study paper which required students to respond to materials and situations by performing communication tasks. The students had a 48-hour preview of two sets of case study materials – photographs, maps, brochures, diagrams, leaflets, etc. When the students entered the examination room they were presented with two sets of tasks, one relating to Case Study A and one relating to Case Study B. At this point they decided which case study to tackle in the three hours of the examination. Paper 2 had a 30 per cent weighting or value.

Paper 3 – a project. Students registered their project in October of the second year of their 'A' level study; the project was completed by May of the second year of study, just before they sat Papers 1 and 2. The project registration had to specify the actual thing that was to be created – a guidebook, a report, a video, a photographic exhibition, whatever. The project had to have a purpose: at registration students had to detail the aims and objectives of the completed project; the project's audience (defined as demographically precisely as possible); the project's resources; and the provisional means of testing the effectiveness of the realised project. The process of working on the project was recorded in a reflective log/commentary, which was produced while working on the project and which had to have some kind of summative, evaluative piece written at end of whole process. Paper 3 had a 30 per cent weighting or value.

Paper 4 – the project's oral. This was an oral presentation made to an audience of the student's peers and two teachers (and for a small sample of students an external moderator appointed by the AEB to attend orals for the purpose of standardisation of internally awarded marks in terms of both the examination centre and across all candidates for the examination). Visual and graphic aids could and would be used. The oral usually consisted of up to twenty minutes of presentation and up to ten minutes of question and answers between the student presenter and their audience. Paper 4 had a 10 per cent weighting or value.

Students had to pass all four papers of the 'A' level to be awarded the qualification.

To give you a flavour of the examination papers those first groups of 'A' level students sat here are some questions from the first 'A' level Communication Studies examination Paper 1 from June 1978:

Means of Communication
What means of communication are available to management intent on promoting safety at work?

In your answer, consider the relative effectiveness of your examples.

Theories of Communication
David Gates, of the group Bread, wrote the song 'If' which begins: 'If a picture paints a thousand words, then why can't I paint you? The words would never show the you I've come to know.'

How far does this quotation make sense? Why does the song-writer feel that the words can never show 'the you I've come to know'?

Mass Communication
Discuss the way in which the social and economic expectations of people have been influenced by the media.

Development of Communications
Modern technology has made entertainment abundantly available. Illustrate the effect of that abundance on *one* social institution.

Apart from the slightly pompous tone in the wording of some of the essay titles it's easy to see continuity from this 1978 'A' level examination paper to what's studied and examined in the name of Communication Studies today. What's also clear from these questions specifically and from the syllabus generally was the humanistic bias or orientation of the 'A' level. This was confirmed by the statements the 1978 students made to Dixon and his team about the vocations they were considering: social work, child care, speech therapy, nursing, journalism, and personnel work.

This first version of 'A' level Communication Studies was very prescriptive about what students should know, and was most demanding in terms of the breadth of knowledge demanded of them. As time went on and the syllabus grew in confidence, changes were made to the 'A' level by the AEB and its senior examining personnel. By the mid-1980s the four sections of Paper 1 had been cut to two: Section A, in which students had to write about communication from an explicitly theoretical or conceptual perspective; and Section B, which combined the three old sections. But much of the spirit of the 1978 paper could be detected in the final Paper 1 of the old (pre-Curriculum 2000) 'A' level of June 2001:

Section A
Feedback is a key element in both interpersonal communication and mass communication. Using examples, compare and contrast the contribution which feedback makes to both interpersonal communication and mass communication.

What are the strengths and the weaknesses of the semiotic approach to the study of communication?

Section B
In 1980 Dale Spender claimed that 'language is *not* neutral'. Analyse the relationship between language and social identity.

(You may wish to think about social identity in terms of one or more of the following: age, ethnicity, gender, region, or social class.)

'Everyone in this room is wearing a uniform and don't kid yourselves.'

> Source: Composer, rock musician and guitarist Frank
> Zappa to fans who were jeering security guards at a concert

What contribution is made by non-verbal factors to group membership?

The government's Curriculum 2000 initiative signalled a profound change in the form, content, organisation and assessment of 'A' levels. All UK examining bodies had to submit new specifications (not syllabuses) for their 'A' levels. One of the many results of this initiative was that there was a significant reduction in the number of 'A' levels available to be studied. Communication Studies was one of the first subjects to complete and publish its new specification and one of the first to be approved by the Qualifications and Curriculum Authority (QCA). All the new 'A' levels had to comply with a new modular format. The 'A' level was divided into two parts: the Advanced Subsidiary (AS) qualification of three AS modules; and the full 'A' level qualification achieved by adding the three A2 modules to the three AS modules. For Communication Studies the titles of the six modules were:

AS modules

1 Introducing Communication Practice

2 Texts and Meanings in Communication

3 Themes in Personal Communication

A2 modules

4 Developing Communication Practice

5 Culture, Context and Communication

6 Issues in Communication

The aims of the new 'A' level Communication Studies specification were to:

promote knowledge and understanding of categories, forms and uses of communication;

enhance candidates' personal communication skills;

introduce and develop candidates' skills in critical reading and evaluating the communication products of themselves and others;

develop candidates' reflexive and evaluative skills in relation to personal communication;

develop and enhance candidates' knowledge of the cultural contexts of communication;

develop candidates' awareness of the contested nature of communication practices and theories and the links between them.

We feel that it's possible to detect in this scheme continuity from the 1978 form of the 'A' level as well as evidence of the confidence the subject had about itself, not least in the last aim where students are positively encouraged to be aware of the debates that emanate from both within and outwith the Communication Studies community about the subject itself. Everything was now up for grabs.

The original 'A' level Communication Studies syllabus was never taken by many candidates: its numbers rose steadily from 1978 to the late 1980s to level out at about 6,000. In its new modular format the AS is taken by about 5,000 candidates, and the A2 by about 2,500. It's instructive to read these statistics against the figure of over 50,000 candidates taking 'A' level Media Studies offered by all the UK examining bodies (AQA is the only body to offer 'A' level Communication Studies). Communication Studies is still most demanding in what it asks students to know and do: much of the content of 'A' level Media Studies specifications can be found in the 'A' level Communication Studies specification – and a lot more besides.

Let's now move on to investigate the story of Communication Studies in UK higher education over the same period we have just covered for further education.

Communication Studies in higher education emerged out of at least two strands of thought and study in post-war universities. Within Sociology there was the tradition of Media Sociology, or the Sociology of Mass Communications. It was from this intellectual tradition that the Centre for Mass Communication Research was established at Leicester University in 1966. The other intellectual tradition was English Literature, in the form that eventually mutated into Cultural Studies. The Centre for Contemporary Cultural Studies was opened at Birmingham University in 1963 and had as its first director Richard Hoggart. He had famously written about his life and education in *The Uses of Literacy*, first published in 1958. He was a working-class boy from Leeds who, despite his class origins, went to university; he used his own life story and experiences to reflect on culture as a whole way of life (while bemoaning the Americanisation of British working-class life). The work of the Centre (or CCCS as it quickly became known) was hugely informed by Hoggart's own work and analysis, as well as by Raymond Williams' work. Williams had used reflections on his Welsh upbringing to come to similar conclusions about culture to Hoggart's. The strain of cultural pessimism in Hoggart's and Williams' work constituted a kind of continuation of that pessimism about popular culture to be found in earlier writers such as Matthew Arnold, the poet T. S. Eliot and the literary critic F. R. Leavis.

When Stuart Hall succeeded Hoggart as director of CCCS, the Centre became more influenced by sociologists such as Peter Berger and Erving Goffman, as well as structuralist Marxists such as Louis Althusser, structuralist anthropologists such as Claude Lévi-Strauss, semioticians such as Roland Barthes and Umberto Eco, and cultural and ideological critics such as Antonio Gramsci and Michel Foucault. Just as Hoggart's life and work informed and guided the work of CCCS in its early days, so too did Hall's life and work inform and guide the work of CCCS in its maturity. Hoggart's northern working-class origins helped determine not only what was studied but how it was studied in a discipline he initially argued could be called 'Literature and Cultural Studies'. That is to say, the life experiences of people who consumed culture were as valid as objects of study as the cultural products themselves. In a similar fashion, Hall's experiences as a Jamaican-born graduate of Oxford University helped further enrich and diversify the range of objects the CCCS's researchers worked on. As it developed, the CCCS's work became focused on symbolic organisation and symbolic processes. Whilst Leicester opted for a political economy analysis of the influence and effects of consumption of mass communication (a mainstream sociological approach), Birmingham moved into critical cultural theory and analysis. What was clearly highlighted by the work of the two centres was the inability of traditional disciplines to analyse expanding media forms and industries, expanding public communication and new perspectives drawn in the main from mainland Europe. The only way in which these could be accommodated into analysis and incorporated into higher education programmes was by forging new interdisciplinary approaches.

As with further education it was structural changes in UK higher education in the 1970s that assisted the development of Communication Studies as a discipline. The higher education sector was greatly expanded by the formation of the polytechnics. They were created by mergers and upgradings of Colleges of Advanced Technology, Colleges of Technology, Teacher Training Colleges and Art Schools. They were intended to be 'equal to but different from' the universities and to provide courses for students in new subjects, often with a strong practical or vocational orientation in new and emerging industries. The character of the polytechnics' degrees was that they would be 'applied' as opposed to 'pure'. The interdisciplinary character of Communication Studies meant that it was made for undergraduate studies in the polytechnics. And the polytechnics had the appropriate mix of staff who could come together to deliver such a programme. As John Corner puts it: 'A three year programme of work around "communication" could be delivered by a disparate group of Arts and Social Science Staff, only a small group of whom required specialist media interests or knowledge of that specific intellectual context surrounding analysis of the media within British culture' (Corner 1998: 4–5).

Undergraduate degrees in the polytechnics were not awarded by the polytechnics themselves but were made by the Council for National Academic Awards (CNAA). By the early 1970s CNAA had created a panel for Communication Studies and it validated the submissions made by teams of staff from key institutions such as Sunderland Polytechnic (now University of Sunderland), the Polytechnic of Central London (now Westminster University), Portsmouth Polytechnic (now Portsmouth University), Sheffield City Polytechnic (now Sheffield Hallam University) and the Lanchester Polytechnic (now Coventry University). At this time the preferred title of undergraduate degree programmes was Communication Studies, but the perspectives ushered into higher education by the centres at Leicester and Birmingham Universities were soon to have quite an effect on both the titles and the content of undergraduate work in this area. While in the late 1970s and the early 1980s the Cultural Studies perspective had been felt to be too 'demandingly abstract and critique-driven to act as the designator of undergraduate studies' (Corner 1998: 7–8), by the early 1990s a softened version of Cultural Studies had become a 'term of institutional convenience to describe an Arts-based mix of studies in which issues of contemporary social change, including those surrounding the media, figured prominently' (Corner 1998: 8). Additionally, UK higher education institutions looked at their further education neighbours who were experiencing (and continue to experience) a massive expansion in Media Studies programmes during the 1990s and decided to make the investments in plant, premises and personnel necessary for the offering of vocationally-oriented Media Studies programmes. In that way UK higher education opened up a still debated divide between what are commonly termed Media Studies and Media Production programmes, where the Studies version concentrates on academic analysis and the Production version concentrates on vocational preparation. Indeed, this divide resembles the division we noted earlier between Communication Studies and Communication Skills.

Of course, this shift in course titles, and the increasing prevalence of Media Studies and Cultural Studies as cover-all programme titles, have ushered in all manner of problems in terms of perception and status. Corner neatly summarises a key dilemma: 'Whilst in the 1970s Communication Studies could be defended or criticised solely in terms of its academic components, it is increasingly the case that Media Studies in the 1990s is discussable only in terms of its career 'promise' and the potential fraudulence of this' (Corner 1998: 24). His response to this can be seen as a call to arms to return to the simple – and less problematic term:

Allowing for a certain arbitrariness in the way in which departments and programmes have come to be named in Britain, a return to the designation Communication Studies to signal a more inclusive and academic setting for teaching about the media might be a great aid in defence and development. (Corner 1998: 31–2)

In 1992 the distinction between universities and polytechnics in terms of their names and their degree-awarding powers was abolished. The so-called 'binary divide' between universities and polytechnics was no longer relevant as it had become increasingly difficult to find a meaningful distinction between the two types of higher education providers. Many of the 'old' universities had embraced the new disciplines; and many of the 'new' polytechnics had established themselves as research-oriented, traditionally the preserve of 'old' universities. Although many commentators routinely employ the terms 'old' and 'new' to differentiate between the pre- and post-1992 universities, for many undergraduate students the distinctions are historical if not mythical. In a buyers' market students want to study in those universities that will teach the subjects they want to study with the resources – human, physical, technical and historical – that they expect. Unfortunately, one of the impacts of the collapsing of the 'binary divide' has been that applicants for Communication Studies or Communication Studies-related courses are faced with the difficult choice of going to universities that are longer established in the field, are better equipped to teach the subject and have more experienced staff, or going to universities that enjoy higher profiles and higher status.

It is unlikely that the next decade will witness a rise in the number of programmes that use the pure and simple title BA Communication Studies, but it is likely that the word 'Communication' will appear in more degree names. In addition, we would point out that the current proliferation of degree titles is unlikely to decline and there is likely to be less and less transparency in actual degree titles; clarity will only ever be found by examining the precise course content of those degrees. It's also the case that Communication Studies will continue to play a key role within other degree programmes in both the name of specific modules and in the importation of its key themes into more traditional programmes – what we might call the Trojan Horse School of Communication Studies. It would be too grand (and probably untenable) to claim that Communication Studies was solely responsible for the changes in UK undergraduate degree programmes as diverse as English, Geography, Psychology and Sociology, but we would remind you of Robert Eaglestone's observations we quoted in our Introduction. He pointed to how doing English had shifted from responding to the text to working with literary theory; it's impossible not to detect the influence of Communication Studies on the seismic changes in UK higher education in the past forty years.

We would further point out that it has been Communication Studies that has been responsible for the increased acknowledgement of students' contributions to their studies. Long gone are the days when university lecturers imperiously handed down their nuggets of wisdom from Olympian heights to students who were totally baffled by the absence of recognition of their own lives and experiences in what they were taught and how they were taught it. To start from where students are rather than from where lecturers would like them to be is now a broadly accepted pedagogic position in arts, humanities and social science education in UK higher education. The experience of the musician and cultural critic Pat Kane exemplifies many of these themes: the acknowledgement of students' prior cultural experience, and the inclusion of Communication Studies-type modules in traditionally titled undergraduate degree programmes. He took a BA in English Literature and Language from Glasgow University in the early 1980s and graduated in 1985. In April 1990 he was inaugurated as Rector of Glasgow University (the students' voted choice of Rector). In his inaugural speech he reflected on his undergraduate studies and the cultural background that motivated and prepared him for this course:

I entered University as a child of the television age; my formative experiences are as much Doctor Who and The Flintstones as they are Robert Louis Stevenson and *Lord of the Flies*. If people of my generation have any common or shared sense, it is their sensitivity to the conventions and themes of broadcast television. The course I chose in my first year that seemed to address this experience was Film and Television Studies.

The course was a revelation: interdisciplinary, eclectic, it revealed what had seemed the most lowly of media to be an incredibly complex phenomenon. Theoretical reasoning was often the only way to open out the workings of this previously most banal of cultures; I learned to apply an understanding of economics, technology, psychology, cultural analysis, politics, history to any particular work or situation, trying always to advance on several disciplinary fronts at once.

(Kane 1992: 193)

Of course, one person's interdisciplinary approach is another person's disciplinary confusion or incoherence. It's probably the very interdisciplinary character of Communication Studies in further and higher education that still puzzles or frustrates some commentators. In an otherwise most complimentary review of *Communication Studies: The Essential Introduction* in the *Times Education Supplement* Laurence Alster characterised the AQA's 'A' level Communication Studies specification as a 'dog's breakfast . . . some sociology mixed with social psychology plus a smidgen of management studies with the occasional dash of history' (*TES* 22 February 2002).

We don't feel that this is a fair or accurate characterisation of the 'A' level specification, but do feel that its being so characterised is an index of how some commentators can think about and talk about Communication Studies only in terms of other disciplines. That might be the fault of Communication Studies itself: it sometimes wants to characterise itself as a battlefield where all comers can take issue with its subject, its objects and its methods; at other times it wants to characterise itself as a stable discipline with a long and venerable history; and at other times still it gets nervous about itself and refers to its studies within the framework of other disciplines (as late as the early 1990s Coventry Polytechnic's BA Communication Studies programme – one of the UK's first such undergraduate programmes – featured compulsory first year modules with titles such as Sociology of the Media and Psychology of Communication.

It might be somewhat confusing to end this chapter on a less than definite note; but to do otherwise would be to misrepresent Communication Studies. It's better to think about Communication Studies in a 'both/and' framework rather than an 'either/or' one. That is to say: if you're looking for an undisputable, absolutely one thing or the other definition of Communication Studies, you've chosen the wrong subject. If, on the other hand, you are open and receptive to a position which argues that the only way to understand and to respond to a life experience that is multifaceted, conflicted, fragmented, slippery and fun is by following a programme of study that is similarly multifaceted, conflicted, fragmented, slippery and fun, then come on down: welcome to Communication Studies!

2 WHICH THEORY FOR COMMUNICATION STUDIES?

This chapter introduces you to two key approaches that have been developed to study Communication. It looks at the process and semiotic schools of communication thought. It comes with the caution that the methods used to do Communication Studies have evolved and changed over the years. To illustrate these changing perspectives the study of film as a form of mass communication is examined. In this chapter a number of key theorists who have influenced communication theory are briefly mentioned. Their ideas and their implications for Communication Studies are explained in more detail in chapters 4 and 5. You would imagine that an introductory guide to Communication Studies would be able to offer an easy and succinct definition of the subject. But it's not that easy. John Fiske admits as much in the first sentence of his *Introduction to Communication Studies*: 'Communication is one of those human activities that everyone recognises but few can define satisfactorily' (Fiske 1990: 1). If you examine the history of those subjects which most people think are solid, respectable well-established disciplines, you might be surprised to discover that they haven't always enjoyed such status, and surprised too to discover that they haven't always enjoyed a fixed definition. In other words, they have been in a state of flux (or development). Their journey from being a subject not deemed worthy of study to being a fringe area of study only grudgingly accepted by the academic community to an accepted area of study has often been long and arduous. For example, the study of English Literature is only a relatively recent addition to the curriculum of British universities. Barely one hundred years have passed since the study of English

Literature was introduced to the University of Cambridge. So it shouldn't be surprising that a subject which has been part of UK universities' curriculum offer for less than fifty years and which is so broad in its scope should be so difficult to define.

What we can do is examine various definitions of Communication Studies and try to contextualise those in terms of the history of the discipline and of its development and its influences. When the Associated Examining Board (AEB) first published its 'A' level Communication Studies syllabus it provided the following definition: 'A study of the arts, practices and media of communication, involving the formulating, gathering, presenting, receiving and interpretation of ideas, information and attitudes'. While we might find it difficult to relate this definition to what we might find published in university prospectuses or in Communication Studies student handbooks today it does represent a fair summary of some of the positions we identified in the first chapter of this book. In the mid-1970s, when the 'A' level syllabus was first published, many people actively involved in teaching Communication Studies in colleges and universities were working inside that kind of model or paradigm of the subject. That is, the strong influence of the US Communication Arts or Speech Communication programmes was still felt. For many teachers Communication Studies equalled Communication Skills. Many students who took Communication Studies courses did so because they felt there was an acute vocational orientation to them. And the majority of teachers who taught Communication Studies in the UK in the mid-1970s were themselves not the products of undergraduate Communication Studies: they had graduated in subjects such as Economics, Literature, Psychology or Sociology, and had taught themselves Communication Studies. In other words, although they were untrained they were most enthusiastic about teaching the subject. But, as we noted from John Corner's remarks in *Communication Studies in the UK*, many early undergraduate Communication Studies programmes were staffed by lecturers from a number of arts, humanities and social science disciplines who were brought together to deliver this interdisciplinary or cross-disciplinary programme of study. As such they did not have a home within their universities. And many colleagues in universities were quite scathing about the subject and its staff. In some universities, and in many colleges, the management approach to staffing Communication Studies programmes was to carve up the syllabus into what were perceived as its constituent parts (that bit's Literature, that bit's Sociology, that bit's Psychology, that bit's Management Theory, and so on) and teachers from those disciplines were assigned to teach the course in a distinctly compartmentalised fashion. It wasn't out of the ordinary for those staff never to meet to discuss the overall picture as far as delivery of the whole course was concerned.

In terms of theory this version (or vision) of the subject emerged out of what we call the Process School of Communication Studies. Although Roman Jakobson and colleagues in the Moscow Linguistic Circle had produced early models of the communication process based on language functions, it is generally agreed that the first widely circulated theorisation about the communication process in the English-speaking world was that devised by Claude Shannon and Warren Weaver. Writing in the July and October 1948 issues of the *Bell Technical Journal*, Shannon offered his Mathematical Theory of Communication. The two papers were revised and published in book form the following year, together with commentary and exposition by Warren Weaver. Shannon was working in the area of telecommunications and was concerned to offer a model that would both explain the process of telecommunication and help telecommunication engineers solve problems in the transmission of information. Shannon and Weaver represented the communication process like this:

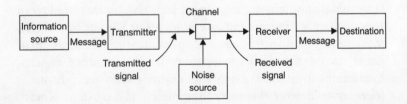

Using the Mathematical Model they took the communication process to function as follows. The information source is taken to be that point in the whole communication process where messages are assumed to originate. At the information source there exists any number of signs. The purpose of these signs is to communicate information. Messages are formed where selective action is brought to bear on a number of signs and where they are ordered into a message. For a communication to take place this message must be amplified by a transmitter such that it achieves a physical form; that is, it becomes a signal. The signal itself must then be transmitted by means of a channel. The transmitted signal arrives at a receiver where the physical form of the signal can be translated back into the original impulse at the physical receiver. The message is now taken to have arrived at its destination and communication is said to have been achieved. Finally, because Shannon wished to give an account of how telecommunication could be subject to disturbances, he inserted a noise source which could intrude into the communication channel. He defined noise as any extraneous signal or information which did not form part of the original message from the information source. Not only did the introduction of a noise source into his communication model explain how the quality of communication could be diminished or reduced, or in any other way made less effective, it also enabled a mathematical value to be placed on the noise source. By doing this telecommunication engineers were able to establish by how much the transmitted signal should be boosted to enable it to overcome the noise source and achieve communication.

Although this model was devised mainly as a problem-solving one to enable reductions in the quality of transmission to be eradicated it was immediately taken up and applied to processes of human communication. It's not difficult to see why, as it does have an attractive simplicity to it. And because it conceives of communication as a process, all those theorists who followed in Shannon and Weaver's footsteps are commonly grouped together as members of the Process School of Communication Thought. While many workers in the field of Communication Studies feel that process theories and models are no longer relevant, a surprising number of people still think about communication as a process. At the beginning of her 2002 book *Communicating: The Multiple Modes of Human Interconnection* Ruth Finnegan surveyed a large number of statements defining communication. She published a small sample of these and they numbered sixteen. Some of these statements do not differ hugely from Shannon and Weaver's formulation; others are distinctly different. As Finnegan states: 'We variously envisage communication as container, conduit or transmission; as control; as war; as dance-ritual' (Finnegan 2002: 9). If Finnegan's total number of sixteen definitions of communication sounds too many, compare her findings with those of James Anderson. In his classic study of Communication first published in 1996, Anderson surveyed seven communication textbooks and found 249 separate theories of communication. What is even more alarming about this is that only 22 per cent of all the theories identified appeared in all the books and only 7 per cent appeared in more than three of the textbooks. So maybe it's not at all surprising that communication is distinctly difficult to define given the proliferation of ideas about what it actually is.

Critics of process theories of communication sometimes forget or choose to ignore that many significant amendments and revisions have been made to Shannon and Weaver's basic notion. (Shannon himself was not without the capacity to engage in auto-critique.) Osgood and Schramm's 1954 model constituted a more sophisticated idea of the encoding and decoding capacity of all communicators, offering a serious amendment to the very fixed character of the transmitter and the receiver in Shannon and Weaver's 1949 formulation.

Not only did this theorisation humanise Shannon and Weaver's way of understanding what was essentially a technologically-mediated form of communication, but it also emphasised the multifaceted and multi-functioned character of human beings when they are engaged in communication.

Many histories of theory in Communication Studies are written according to a template where every succeeding model or theory criticises every preceding theory or model – with the

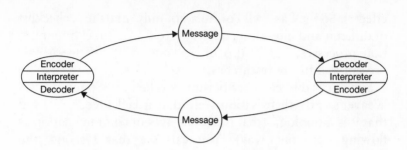

assumption that the new theory or model is truer than the earlier theory or model. Whilst some later theories and models do offer greater insights into human communication and do offer refinements of cruder formulations, it would be a mistake to think that all later models are more accurate and all early models are inaccurate or incomplete. Many early theories and models continue to provide insights into processes of communication. We would argue that this is the case with what is now routinely referred to as the Lasswell Formula. Devised by the American sociologist Harold Lasswell in 1948, it isn't really a formula but rather is a set of questions which it is useful to ask about communication.

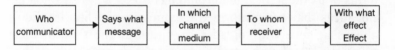

Whilst this formulation might seem unduly simple and reductionist by today's standards actually getting appropriate answers to these questions can prove difficult even today. What's more, the five elements present in the Lasswell Formula correspond with those aspects of human communication on which different communication researchers have focused. Some researchers have concentrated on the producers or originators of communication (who?); some on communication messages and the contents of communications (says what?); some on communication engineering and processes of communication (in which channel?); some on receivers and processes of reception (to whom?); and some on the effects of communication, particularly mass communication (with what effect?). So the Lasswell Formula not only offers us a checklist of difficult and interesting questions to ask about communication processes, but it also offers connections between past present and future researches.

Some of the early criticisms levelled at Shannon and Weaver's early theorisation were that it lacks feedback, and that it is monologic (that is, it conceives of communication as flowing only one way). You can see that Osgood and Schramm's 1954 model constituted an attempt to provide a dialogic as opposed to monologic account of human communication. In 1966 Melvin DeFleur produced a very detailed development and revision of the Shannon and Weaver model which sought to incorporate many of the criticisms made of it. DeFleur hoped that his expanded and developed model would satisfactorily explain processes of feedback, the transmitting and receiving functions of people, and the use of mass communication devices. The point of all this is that process theorists never sat back in the confidence that they had produced the definitive model; rather, they continued to work on their theorisations, refining, rejecting and developing them.

An irony of Communication Studies is that its history in terms of its theoretical underpinnings isn't always chronological. Ideas that have informed Communication Studies didn't always achieve widespread recognition at the time of their original formulation, and they didn't always achieve that recognition at the same time everywhere. So it is the case with semiotics and structuralism. Although the theorisations that informed the second wave of communication thought were formulated before the publication of those process models which informed the second wave of Communication thought, their impact on thinking about Communication appeared to be critical rather than fundamental. Semiotic ideas were first devised over fifty years before the first process models, but they weren't known or discussed outside the world of academic linguistics. Ferdinand de Saussure's ideas about general linguistics, first aired in his lectures at the end of the nineteenth century, did not achieve significant recognition until the late 1950s – and then only in France and then only through the work of Roland Barthes. And it took until the 1970s for those ideas to make the journey into the world of Anglophone theory in the form of de Saussure's general linguistics, Marx and Engels' historical materialism, and Freud's psychoanalysis. In his 1988 novel *Nice Work* David Lodge neatly summarised the impact of the arrival of this heady mixture of perspectives and analytical methods on UK higher education. He lists those perspectives and methods and atomises their disruptive impact:

> structuralism and poststructuralism, semiotics and deconstruction, new mutations and graftings of psychoanalysis and Marxism, linguistics and literary criticism. The more conservative dons viewed these ideas and their proponents with alarm, seeing in them a threat to the traditional values and methods of literary scholarship.
>
> (Lodge 1988: 46)

All the -isms and -ics rehearsed here might be unfamiliar to you now but they won't be once you've read Chapters 4 and 5 of this book but what's important here is that you pick up on the way in which academics have reacted negatively to new or radical perspectives.

In UK Communication Studies the move from studying Communication from a process perspective to studying Communication from a semiotic perspective marked a significant shift. Much of the work undertaken within a process framework had an acute focus on human communication processes. It was conducted in the belief that human communication could and should be better understood – and that such an understanding would lead to the improvement of communication between people. The work was carried out inside distinctly logical frameworks where clearly stated goals were offered and improvements in the effectiveness of human communication were measured against those goals. Within the world of process thought there was a remarkable degree of consensus about the whole project of the study of Communication. Further, there was a large degree of agreement that the project was being conducted in the spirit of scientific discovery. Indeed, the popular appeal of process work can probably be ascribed to its being conducted in a scientific vein. It's quite possible that the scientific flavour of those early process studies was key to their shaping the dominant paradigm in the early Communication Studies teaching in UK further and higher education. And it's perfectly possible to argue that the shift from a process perspective to a semiotic perspective is a reflection of changing times and changing cultural perspectives. It's possible to read the UK in the 1960s and the 1970s as an historical era characterised by a belief in science (and the capacity of science to make a better society) and by a belief in consensus. And it's possible to read the UK in the 1980s and the 1990s as an historical era characterised by a loss of belief in science (or, at the very least, *hard* science) and by loss of consensus (who is the 'we' in so much of contemporary rhetoric?). Ultimately, it could well be the case that Communication Studies' turning away from hard science and the search for consensus is but one index of the discipline's greater belief in itself as more hesitant, partial, and tentative. (To be certain, to try to be consensual now would be to commit oneself to being out of step with the spirit of our times.)

We've made brief reference to semiotics in the previous chapter of this book and have introduced you to the idea that the process and the semiotic constitute two contrasting or opposed ways of looking at or studying Communication. We will soon explain some of the ways in which semiotics had an impact on Communication Studies but we need to offer two admonitions here: (1) it's as impossible to precisely date when the semiotic perspective overtook the process perspective as it is to date when the postmodern era succeeded the modern era; and (2) we must remind ourselves that although the process *succeeded* the semiotic in chronological terms, it *preceded* the semiotic in terms of being a defining perspective for the formal study of Communication.

Although it is convenient to talk about the process and the semiotic as constituting two distinct, coherent and whole schools of thought the reality is quite different. There was, and there continues to be, divergence of opinion within these two schools of thought. Moreover, we have been using the two terms to stand for bodies of thought that are far more diverse than those two short, simple words might lead you to believe. For example, we have been using 'semiotics' to stand for what we earlier characterised as a heady mixture of general linguistics, historical materialism and psychoanalysis. We don't mean to claim that they are all interchangeable; but if we start using the term 'structuralist' we would be moving towards one word that has come to stand for that combination of perspectives and methods. What is indisputable is that the widespread adoption and use of this combination of perspectives and methods by UK academics in the mid to late 1970s lead to a fundamental re-defining of Communication Studies. There's a way of reading the study of Communication from the mid-1970s onwards as something of a battlefield on which an old guard and a new order were engaged in bloody struggle. (That might seem like hyperbole to you now, but we assure you that academics are capable of joining battle about and over what might seem to academic outsiders to be trivial or invisible distinctions.)

We deal with semiotics and structuralism in detail in Chapter 5 The Communication Studies Toolkit, but we need to take a brief look at some of the basic principles of that approach here. In this way we can begin to demonstrate how viewing Communication from a semiotic (and, ultimately, structuralist) perspective constituted such a significant departure from the process perspective, a way of moving away from what Ruth Finnegan has characterised as the model assumed in 'accounts in the standard social science literature' with its emphasis on ' " information", "messages", "codes" and "meanings" ' (Finnegan 2002: 9).

Key to understanding semiotics is the greater role it accorded the receiver or the reader. In semiotic terms messages are not sent; rather, meanings are generated. The reader of a communication is as responsible for its meanings as is the originator. Furthermore, as everything we credit with the capacity to communicate is created by human beings, all communication is based on arbitrary systems of connection and all communication is open to interpretation. In this way a picture of a more empowered receiver or reader emerges: no more are they conceived of as the passive receiver of messages – now they are at the very least part-creator of the meanings generated by these communicative interactions.

The Swiss linguist Ferdinand de Saussure was responsible for pointing out the fundamentally arbitrary character of all communication. He proposed that the basic unit of communication was the sign, and he further proposed that the sign was composed of two elements.

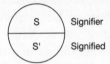

where the signified is the object we refer to when we communicate verbally or in writing and the signifier is the spoken or written word we use to refer to that object. Not only did de Saussure propose that the signifier itself was an arbitrary collection of noises (in the air) or shapes (on the page) but he also proposed that the relationship, the connection between the two elements (the signifier and the signified), was itself arbitrary. There is no logical, rational, or necessary connection between the two. They are related only by repetition and convention: everyone else in society uses this convention so too do we for fear of not getting on, for fear of being ostracised by our fellow citizens, for fear of failing to communicate.

Working at much the same time as de Saussure but wholly unaware of his work was the American philosopher and logician Charles A. Peirce. He also proposed that communication was carried out by the use of signs but his conception of the sign was a little more complicated than de Saussure's. He proposed that there were three elements present in any use of the sign.

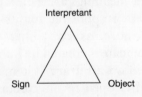

In many ways this takes further the idea of an empowered reader, as well as cutting loose the text from its acute and unique relationship with its originator. In Peirce's sign there are three elements present: the object, the thing being referred to; the interpretant, or the mental concept of the object as used by the reader; and the sign itself, not an immutable thing but something which is inflected in its every use. At the very least this points us to the notion that the sign as used by its originator will not be the exactly the same as the sign as used by its reader. Thus a more active and dynamic notion of the sign emerged.

Now let's look at some of the ramifications semiotics and structuralism had on the study of Communication in UK higher education. Much of what follows in the rest of this chapter will use the study of film as a site where the impact of these new perspectives may be explored and understood.

In the study of film it's possible to detect the process and semiotic perspectives expressed as *auteurist* and structuralist positions.

Derived from the French word for 'author' the belief in an *auteur* system has quite a long history. In literary criticism there is a long-held belief that all the meanings to be derived from a novel, play or poem have been built into the text by their authors, and that the only work a reader has to do is to dig out those meanings. In other words the author reigns supreme, all-powerful and all-knowing about their text, and the role of the reader is to appreciate how clever the author has been. Writing in *Rolling Stone* in July 1970 Greil Marcus succinctly summarised both this position and its ramifications for the study of texts:

> '*Auteur*' means, literally, 'author,' and in America the word has come to signify a formula about films: movies (like books) are made by 'authors,' i.e. directors, This has led to the dictum which tends to affirm the following: movies are about the personality of the director, We should judge a movie in terms of how well the *auteur* has 'developed his personality' in relation to previous

films. His best film is that which most fully presents the flower of his personality. (Marcus in Hedin 2004: 89)

More recently Wally Olins has written about branding in a distinctly *auteurist* fashion:

> The brand has become so significant a phenomenon of our time that it is almost impossible to express any ideas, or even delineate personalities, without branding them. Even people who would shudder at the thought that they had anything to do with branding are trapped by it. Woody Allen's movies are as strongly branded as Disney's, although he wouldn't thank anyone for saying so. The plots, the characters, the camera angles, the music all characterize the Woody Allen brand. (Olins 2003: 23)

Whether you choose to call this *auteurism* or branding doesn't matter; what both terms have in common is the idea of there being a definitive signature on mass cultural products. (What's notable is that although thirty-three years separate the pronouncements of Marcus and Olins, it's difficult to discern any real difference between them.)

Magazines produced for film fans are almost as old as the medium itself but in the UK in the late 1950s and early 1960s significant changes began to be obvious in these magazines' content. Magazines such as *Films and Filming*, which had been first published in 1954, ceased to content themselves with publishing such items as film reviews and location reports about films made in the UK and the US. *Films and Filming* began featuring items about European films, which appeared to be infinitely more serious than UK and US films; and it began to feature lengthy ruminations on film as a mass communication medium by earnest critics such as Raymond Durgnat.

Whilst magazines such as *Films and Filming* never identified themselves fully with the *auteurist* position other than in the way that in everyday conversation about films people still refer to 'Hitchcock's films' or 'Scorsese's films' other magazines were not so shy. *Movie* magazine had been founded by a group of British students who were excited about film despite the fact that they were unable to study it formally at university. They were excited about the New Wave of French film-makers. Following the lead of writers on the French film magazine *Cahiers du Cinema* they set about the project of discovering some of the secret histories of US pulp films where unacknowledged geniuses were quietly working inside the film studio factory system building up career-length bodies of work; in other words, they sought to reveal unrecognised *auteurs*. Amongst the writers who worked at *Cahiers du Cinema* were Claude Chabrol, Jean-Luc Godard, Jacques Rivette, Eric Röhmer, and François Truffaut. All of them subsequently became prominent film-makers. One way of looking at their careers is that they used *Cahiers du Cinema* to publish their blueprints for the films they wanted to make – and then went on to make them. And in so doing founded a school of film criticism; indeed it was Truffaut's 1954 publication of his essay 'Une Certaine Tendance du Cinéma Français' in *Cahiers du Cinema* that is widely credited with initiating the discussion about a 'politique des auteurs' that led in turn to the widespread adoption of *auteurist* thought in the study of film. Amongst *Movie*'s founders and writers were V. F. Perkins, Mark Shivas and Robin Wood. Whilst Shivas established a reputation as a film and television producer. Perkins and Wood became influential in establishing film as an object of study in UK universities and in promoting the *auteurist* position within those studies.

First as a film critic and then as a film-maker Jean-Luc Godard admired the work of US film-makers such as Howard Hawks, Anthony Mann, Vincente Minnelli and Nicholas Ray. In their time none of these film-makers was regarded as a towering figure of film or as the unheralded poet Godard and his associates at *Cahiers du Cinema* felt them to be. But they did offer Godard and other French film-makers models of production and efficiency when it came to actually making films. Further, they offered a certain kind of revisionist aesthetic in terms of making films drawn from popular, not to say pulp, fiction. Made between *Le Mépris* and *Alphaville* Godard's

1964 film *Bande À Part* can be read in part as his homage to 1940s Hollywood pulp film-making. Godard is reported to have said that to make such a film 'all you need is a girl and a gun' (the phrase itself echoing the title of Willard Weiner's 1952 Avon pulp paperback *Four Boys a Girl and a Gun*). Even by the technologically enhanced standards of today's film-making the first few minutes of *Bands A Part*'s opening sequence are quite breathtaking: a jigsaw puzzle set of characters appears which assemble to form the film's title (*Bande A Part*); this is rapidly followed by an almost subliminally edited collage of the lead actors' faces accompanied by honky tonk piano music; then, abruptly, it cuts to a Parisian street scene where the music fades to location street sounds; most of the production credits appear quickly, presented in brutally brief industrial terms; then the 'real' sounds fade as Michel Legrand's elegant widescreen jazz rises up on the soundtrack, and the film's final credit appears:

JEANLUC
CINEMA
GODARD

There are a couple of minutes of apparently establishing dialogue between the two lead male characters intercut with a voiceover that appears to provide the viewer with background information about the characters, but then, nearly eight minutes into the film, the set of distancing devices from the title sequence is consolidated by a voiceover which runs: 'The story till now, for people who've come in late: Three weeks ago . . . a hoard of money . . . an English class . . . a house by the river . . . a starry-eyed girl.' This is the ultimate strategy of distanciation: if you as a viewer were in any doubt that you were watching a film you are not now.

The irony of Godard being championed as an *auteurist* giant is that he is, at one and the same time, a suitable case for being read as an author and as a maker of films who explicitly invited his audience into participating in the construction of his films' meanings whilst functioning as an avowedly anti-*auteurist* film-maker in the sense of pursuing an anti-Romantic work aesthetic. In *auteurist* terms his films bear the signature of a film-maker of such startling originality that they can still be run today to offer object lessons in film technique for upcoming generations of film-makers, for young directors who want to be themselves rather than pale imitations of members of the directors' hall of fame. Indeed, every film that Quentin Tarantino has made since *Pulp Fiction* in 1994 have been credited to the production company Band Apart – both a play on the original French title of Godard's film (a slightly better translation than *The Outsiders* which *Bande À Part* usually appears under) and an acknowledgement that he owes as much to French New Wave film-makers as he does to Marvel Comics for his inspiration in making films. Godard is reputed to have reacted to this homage by commenting, 'He'd have done better to have given me some money'. But this apparently dour reaction on Godard's part is fundamental to his anti-Romantic, materialist approach, where he has consistently sought to defuse or derail audiences' potential veneration of him. Two examples of his approach will suffice here. Once asked by a critic about how he had achieved a particularly telling emotional effect in one of his films, Godard replied in strictly technical (materialist) terms: his cinematographer Raoul Coutard had used a specific camera, a specific film stock and a specific lighting set-up. In other words, the emotional response is a particularly bourgeois indulgence and all the effects created by the viewing of films by large audiences in the dark can be ascribed to purely technical causes. The second example is more famous and was once used by comedians to point to the ostensible incoherence of Godard's film-making methods. Interviewed when visiting London to coincide with the UK release of one of his early films, Godard was interviewed and reported as saying that he thought that films should have a beginning, a middle and an end – but not necessarily in that order. Although Godard was reviled and ridiculed for this statement at the time, now it can be read as offering a way of crediting audiences with the capacity to play an active role in the construction of films' meanings and as an astute foretaste of things to come in cinema.

The mention of Tarantino is not gratuitous for he presents as much of an interesting problem for theory now as Jean-Luc Godard did forty years ago. In the 1920s theatre audiences had rioted at Bertolt Brecht's plays where his alienating or distancing devices had included a cast of self-conscious actors who stepped out of character to comment on the action of the play or to point to the parallels/connections between what was taking place on stage and what was happening in society at large – or on their doorstep. Godard's use of a distancing voice over in *Bande À Part* had served a similar function. And Tarantino has used similar devices to comment on the mechanics of bourgeois drama where actors remind audiences that they are indeed watching a film. Let's take two examples from *Kill Bill Vol. 2*. At the beginning of the film the bride (Uma Thurman) makes a speech to camera where she refers to herself and her actions in the final act of *Kill Bill Vol. 1* in a self-conscious fashion: 'When I woke up I went on what the movie advertisements refer to as a roaring rampage of revenge'. The distanciation is compounded by Tarantino's use of monochrome film stock (in a film that frequently uses different film stocks and colour processes, Manga cartoons, and old vinyl soundtracks (where you the viewer/listener can clearly hear it's sourced from vinyl) to shock the audience out of any prospect of getting sucked into viewing of the film as naturalistic). And then towards the end of the film Bill (David Carradine) delivers a speech which serves a similar distancing function where he anticipates what is left to happen 'before this tale of bloody revenge reaches its climax'. This is self-conscious film-making where characters behave in a self-conscious fashion, stepping out of role and commenting upon their characters and the film's action in a fashion that both Brecht and Godard would recognise.

What's fascinating about the above passage is that it illustrates how difficult it can be to disentangle the *auteurist* and structuralist positions, how it is possible to analyse and appreciate the work of Godard and Tarantino from both *auteurist* and semiotic perspectives. Although he was late in coming to using semiotics to analyse film (having been a member of the group of *Movie* writers who had previously pioneered *auteurism*) Robin Wood offered this assessment of *Bande À Part* in 1984; he admired the film for the way in which 'the traditional relationship between signifier and signified shows a continuous tendency to come adrift, so that the *process of narration* (which mainstream cinema strives everywhere to conceal) becomes foregrounded' (Wood in Lyon 1984: 221). This exemplifies a dilemma for Communication theory: the impossibility of forging one complete, coherent, all-explaining body of theory. In assessing Godard Wood uses semiotic terminology and perspectives to praise him as an all-powerful and all-knowing *auteur*. Perhaps this is why it is surprising to see academics reacting negatively to attempts to forge new combinations of perspectives and methodologies where single bodies of thought insufficiently explain the complex character of contemporary texts.

In light of what we've just said it might appear odd to look back at the impact of semiotics and structuralism on UK higher education but it can be instructive in understanding how different groups of scholars have come to adopt specific positions and how they have defended those positions to the exclusion of all other positions. The film journals *Screen* and *Screen Education* are widely credited with extending the use of semiotics in UK higher education out of the study of language and into the study of film and other processes and practices in mass communication. In the 1970s these journals, together with *Media, Culture and Society* (which was founded in 1979 by staff in the School of Communications at the Polytechnic of Central London), were held to have revolutionised thinking about Communication and Media Studies in UK universities and polytechnics.

Words like 'revolutionised' are now routinely used in all kinds of public fora in a somewhat debased fashion – often by politicians and captains of industry selling so much snakeoil. But notions of 'revolution' and the 'overthrow of the old guard' are not out of order here for that is how this area of academia was genuinely seen: as a war where the stakes were high and where old guard and new order were locked into a battle where only one side could win. Of course, this wasn't a 'real' war but rather was one fought out in the pages of academic journals and learned monographs but for the combatants it was as serious as life. For all the appeal of the new ways of looking at Communication the old guard didn't take it lying down. In the 26 December 1974 edition of *New Society* Peter Wason and Ormond Uren published an article entitled 'The semantics of semiotics', the main thrust of which was to demolish an article by Julia Kristeva published in the *Times Literary Supplement* the previous year. Kristeva is a psychoanalyst who synthesised psychoanalytical and semiotic perspectives with an (implied rather than explicitly stated) feminist critique of the father-oriented dimensions of the work of some of Freud's followers. What Wason and Uran seemed to have difficulty with was the slippery character of the language used by Kristeva. They appeared distinctly unsympathetic to the idea that one might have to use slippery, tentative language to describe things (like communication) that were slippery and tentative themselves.

One of the most virulent attacks on the whole *Screen* and *Screen Education* project was written by Andrew Britton and published in the 1978/79 edition of *Movie*. The *Movie* writers regarded what the *Screen* writers were doing as not being film criticism but a more blatantly ideological project. Although they had embraced *auteur* theory they eschewed theory with a capital T. They resented the intrusion of semiotics, psychoanalysis and ideology into the discussion and appreciation of film for in many ways what they were doing were continuing F. R. Leavis' project of moral criticism through the medium of literature. Hence the title of Britton's piece – 'The Ideology of *Screen*'. In his long article Britton sought to lay bare the influences of the *Screen* writers – Louis Althusser, Jacques Lacan, and Roland Barthes – and to question how and why they were being invoked in the study of film – and by implication communication.

Today it is simply unthinkable that such attacks would be made in the sense that everyone who works within Communication Studies realises that even if they do not agree with all and every formulation of Althusser, Lacan, and Barthes any study of Communication which does not consider the perspectives afforded them by ideology, psychoanalysis, and semiotics would be worthless. It's all the more odd when one considers that much of what Althusser, Lacan and Barthes were saying wasn't *that* new, indeed much of the impact of Althusser can be read as a call to return to Marx, as can much of Lacan be read as a call to return to Freud, and much of Barthes can be read as a call to rediscover de Saussure.

Quite possibly the best answer to the question of which theory should be used to do Communication Studies is that no one theory will do. We ended the previous chapter with the advice that it was better to think about Communication Studies in a 'both/and' framework rather than an 'either/or' framework. And that spirit of 'both/and' doesn't just exist in the moment. As you have seen in this chapter we have shown how some theories (for example, the Lasswell Formula) have been deemed outmoded in the light of more modern theories but we have argued that they can still be applied to specific forms of communication. Further, you have seen how Communication Studies has an odd sense of chronology: although one theory might precede another in historical terms, it succeeds another in terms of being broadcast and widely taken up. Finally, we have to remind ourselves that times change and as times change so too do perspectives. Earlier in this chapter we told you how Jean-Luc Goddard was reported as saying that he thought all films should have a beginning, a middle and an end but not necessarily in that order. By 1994 Quentin Tarantino had done just that with *Pulp Fiction*, where he offered cinema audiences a film that constituted a postmodern playing with conventional notions of time and narrative structure. Yesterday's avant-garde is today's mainstream. Yesterday's extreme and obscure theory is today's commonplace.

3   COMMUNICATION STUDIES NOW

This chapter is intended to give you a flavour of the range of programmes taught under the umbrella term Communication Studies in UK universities. It surveys the many current approaches to and theories about Communication Studies. You are advised that the character of what is actually offered at any given UK university in the name of Communication Studies will be influenced by a number of factors: the history of the subject within that particular institution; the past and current staff who deliver the Communication Studies programme(s); the career trajectories of the staff who deliver the Communication Studies programme(s); and where the institution is located within the UK. We close this chapter with brief career profiles of some recent Communication Studies graduates.

Please note: in this chapter we will start making cross-references to other sections in this book. Where we do this the reference will appear in parenthesis and the title of the section will appear in **bold**.

As you know from chapter 1 Communication Studies has been taught at British universities since the late 1970s. At the same time Media Studies and Cultural Studies were growing rapidly as university disciplines. There is a great deal of overlap between these two areas. They are really best understood not as separate disciplines with different objects of study but as different approaches to the same objects. Courses called Media Studies are likely to concentrate primarily on the analysis and production of media texts such as newspapers, magazines, television and radio programmes, films and Internet texts. Cultural Studies programmes are likely to concentrate more on areas such as the representation and construction of identity, together with considerations about cultural consumption and taste, and issues of gender, ethnicity or ability/disability. Communication Studies courses may be focused more closely on theories of meaning and the study of signs and language. However, all three overlap greatly. You may well find that a course called Media Studies in one university looks remarkably like one called Communication Studies in another. You will also find that more and more universities have hybrid titles for their courses: Communication and Mass Media; English and Communication Studies; or Communication Culture and Media.

This is likely to be further complicated by the increasing tendency of universities to offer titles that incorporate more than one of the terms – for example, Media and Cultural Studies. In each and every case, you need to look at the actual content of the course as set out in the literature and websites published by the institution offering it. Where the same institution offers, say, separate programmes called Media and Communication Studies and Media and Cultural Studies you may expect to identify a difference of emphasis between the programmes broadly in line with the characterisations given above. This is one of the reasons that we strongly advise students to read detailed descriptions of course content before applying for courses (rather than just reading the entry in the university prospectus).

All such courses will involve the study of texts, considered in the broadest sense, including photographs, television programmes, advertisements and sporting events, as well as written or spoken texts. You will be expected to engage critically with these texts – that is, to look not just for their surface meaning but for the codes and nuances that convey deeper meanings.

A significant part of your time as a student of Communication will be spent in this sort of close analysis. For example, in analysing an advertisement for perfume, you may notice that in addition to the obvious message which tells you about a particular brand of fragrance and the images the manufacturer wants you to associate with it (sophistication, glamour or high style), the photograph and the written text combine to mobilise a whole range of cultural assumptions about particular nationalities, about types of female beauty and, indeed, about the character of femininity itself. This is, essentially, what Judith Williamson does in her analysis of the Chanel No. 5 advertisement featuring the French actress Catherine Deneuve, in her classic text, *Decoding Advertisements.*

Similarly, you might be engaged in the study of a news story, looking closely at the way it is constructed and the effect that has on the reader's interpretation of it. Next time you watch the television news, think about the way things and people are described. No doubt you will have heard the saying 'one person's terrorist is another's freedom fighter'. Can you think of alternative ways to describe people that would change the way they are being presented? Consider the emphasis given to different stories. Why does one come first and have a lot of time spent on it when others are dealt with more briefly? Of course, this reflects someone's judgement about their relative importance. But who makes that decision? And why do they make it? Why is it the case that across different television channels' newscasts there's a large degree of agreement about the running order (the order of priority) of any given evening's news stories? Would you have made a different choice?

UK university degree courses are not (yet) like 'A' levels, AVCEs, GNVQs, Scottish Highers or Baccalaureates. All of these have a syllabus or specification written and examined by an outside body so that students at many schools and colleges will study very similar programmes. The syllabus or specification is the same; only the implementation of them will differ from institution to institution. By contrast, each university sets its own syllabus. There is a complex system of inter-university quality control which ensures that all degree courses are broadly equivalent in terms of level of difficulty and achievement and that the content of courses is appropriate to the course title. However, no two degree programmes are the same and there will always be local features that make a course more or less suited to your particular requirements. We strongly advise candidates to visit universities to which they are applying or thinking of applying to discuss with lecturers and especially current students whether the course is what they are looking for. It is a big risk to accept a place at an institution you have not visited; nowadays this would be literally to buy a product unseen and untested.

Because university degree courses are individual each has been shaped, over the years, by the composition and activity of its teachers and students. Indeed, they are likely always to be in a state of flux; this is not only because quality assurance processes in universities insist on constant review and updating, but also because programmes such as Communication Studies are constantly alert and responsive to the changing character of its objects of study. You may confidently expect certain areas of study to be present on all courses with Communication Studies in the title. These will include semiotics (the science of signs and meanings (see **Semiotics**)), textual analysis, visual literacy (see **Visual Rhetorics**), representation and the consumption of media artefacts and texts (for example, television shows, sporting events, celebrity divorces and popular songs).

In addition to these, however, there will be a range of topics which are available because of the particular expertise of teachers within the department. Thus some universities will have greater expertise than others in journalism, some in screen studies (television, film and multimedia) and others in photography or communication design. Where it was once the case that communication and media practitioners used to 'retire' in effect by moving into university teaching after a career in industry, nowadays there is a healthy degree of two-way traffic, with people moving backwards and forwards between university and industry. Moreover, an increasing number of Communication Studies teachers work for half the time in university teaching and half the time in communication and media industries. University lecturers are expected not only to teach but to undertake research so that their teaching is informed by a lively and current knowledge of the contemporary issues and debates in their field.

Communication Studies is a hybrid subject in that it includes both analytical aspects and practical ones. To some extent, of course, all degree courses do this. Whether you study supposedly traditional, long-established, 'academic' subjects like Philosophy or History or go for a more obviously 'vocational' course such as Law or Business Administration, you have a reasonable expectation that you will acquire both knowledge of the subject and a range of relevant skills which will make you attractive to future employers. Going to university should be about more than simply the career you hope to follow when you graduate, but it is a legitimate concern, particularly as students can expect to incur significant levels of debt while studying.

The balance between production-based work (for example, in Public Relations or in Video Production) and work centred on the analysis and criticism of texts and cultural artefacts varies greatly from course to course and institution to institution. Unless you have a very strong conviction that you already know in which direction you want to take your working and studying life, it is a good idea to look for a course that will enable you to get a broad range of skills, knowledge and experience in the first year so that you can make informed choices about the directions in which you want to specialise as time goes on. Some universities organise their Communication Studies programmes on a very prescriptive course basis, where there is little opportunity for students to take option modules; others organise their programmes on a cafeteria basis, where students can pick and mix modules. Neither system is ideal for all students; but students with different degrees of thought developed about how they will fulfil their work and career ambitions will find different programme structures more (or less) appropriate for them. If you have a clear sense of what you want to do, then following a clearly named route or pathway through a degree programme will be more appropriate. If you have no clear sense of what you want to do, then picking and mixing through your undergraduate studies to get the widest possible spread of modules will be more appropriate. (This is another feature of potential courses you should look at before deciding at which university you want to study.)

Another feature which could decide at which university you study Communication is where that university is located.

Historically speaking communication and media industries were located in key UK cities. So students who wanted to maximise their chances of making industry contacts and gaining work placements with prestigious employers tended to take Communication Studies degrees at universities in places like London, Manchester, Birmingham and Bristol. Modern communication and information technology has meant that many organisations no longer have to be located in metropolitan centres like London, but old habits die hard and it is the case that many communication organisations are still located in major UK cities. So, looking to where the university at which you want to study Communication is located geographically is another factor to bear in mind if you have a keen eye on your future career.

It is by no means always the case that the areas of the subject that interest you when starting the course will inevitably be the ones in which you end up doing your best work. University study should be a journey of discovery and you may well discover whole new areas of interest that become your chosen specialism. We have observed, for instance, students who came from a background of studying English Literature who arrived intending to become newswriters, who took an option in photography out of curiosity, and thereafter made that their specialism and career.

If, on the other hand, you are convinced that you know now that you are going to be a film director, a cultural critic or a radio journalist, it is obviously sensible to look for a course with good coverage of that area. Even then, it is a very good idea to take as broad a range of study in your first year as you can. Being a good television producer or radio announcer is not just about knowing about editing technology or microphone technique. Like all degrees, a BA in Communication Studies should indicate not only that you have a body of specialist knowledge but also that you are an educated, cultured and well-rounded person. Because of this, many universities encourage students to take at least one option in their first year in a totally different discipline. Some Communication Studies students take this opportunity to take a related option which they hope will enhance their career profile, such as a modern language or a business skill such as Marketing. Others choose something completely different from their degree subject, such as a History or Fine Art module. In many ways, going completely away from your primary interest with a free choice module can be the most rewarding path to take. Demonstrating to yourself and to others that you have a wide range of knowledge and interests and that your opinions, views and choices are influenced by a broad and general education is as important to your career prospects and your future as practical skills.

Before we close this chapter it is useful to offer some brief profiles of Communication Studies graduates, to see what they are doing with their qualifications, to hear what they have to say about the relevance of their degrees, and to find out what they are doing in their jobs. All of the people profiled here graduated from Coventry University between 2001 and 2004 with BAs in Communication Culture and Media (CCM) and spoke about their work and careers in autumn 2004.

Suzy Davis works for the BBC. She enjoyed a swift upwards career trajectory after completing her studies in 2001. A busy employee she offered this brief précis of her career so far:

'I'll just list my jobs in a kind of CV format for you with a bit of blurb on each.

'Straight after Uni I first worked as a runner for Granada TV – doing general dogsbody stuff.

'Then went to work on *This Morning* as a junior researcher. Over the next three years worked my way up through researcher, assistant producer then a short spell as stand-in producer.

'Then I went off and disappeared for a year in the dirty depths of reality TV, working as a producer on shows like *Fame Academy*, *The Salon* and *The Games*.

'I eventually got bored with that, and decided I wanted to make documentaries; so am now working for the BBC as an assistant producer in the contemporary factual and documentaries department – I have been doing this since the summer.'

Danielle Ellis also graduated in 2001 and currently works as a researcher for Cactus TV. Another very busy television worker, she stole a few moments to offer us her career résumé:

'It's my show day tomorrow, so it's always a bit frantic on prep day!

'After leaving Coventry in 2001, I went home to Bournemouth and got a job working for a tiny, corporate production company called Hallmark Productions.

'I was a good all-rounder – I got the chance to do running, camera work and editing. I stayed there for six months and then whilst working for a freelance director I'd met through Hallmark, I met a presenter who worked at QVC – the shopping channel.

'She passed my CV on, and I was offered a job as a Production Assistant.

'I moved to London and worked there for two years. Whilst at QVC I did a couple of freelance jobs through contacts I'd made, and built up quite a lot of "live" experience.

'I joined Cactus TV and *The Richard & Judy Show* in October 2003 as their Phone Room Co-ordinator.

'I'm still with Cactus, but am now a researcher on the programme.

'I still live in London and couldn't possibly move!

'People have often asked me if I needed my degree in order to get where I am now.

'When I first graduated I wondered this myself – was the debt worth it? My answer now is a definite YES!

'I can honestly say that I wouldn't be at Cactus if I hadn't completed my degree in CCM.'

Another 2001 graduate is Peter Ogden. He now works for Granada Factuals in London as a researcher.

'I worked undercover for a year or so for the *From Hell* series – *Restaurants From Hell*, etc. From there I worked for a couple of independent companies making one-offs and pilots.

'Then I came to *This Morning* a year and a half ago, was made an assistant producer, and in fact last Friday produced my first programme!'

Another 2001 graduate is Susan Poole. In the second year of her undergraduate studies she took a Work Placement module and worked in a prestigious London advertising agency. She moved directly from her undergraduate studies to her current job as a planner in the advertising agency Burkitt DDB. She picks up her story:

'Four years on and I'm still Planning away here at Burkitt DDB, which is a medium-sized advertising agency in London – part of the DDB worldwide network, owned by Omnicom.

'My current clients include: John Lewis Department stores (took them on TV for the first time last year and this year), Bakers Complete Dog Food (the number one company in dry dog food), South West Trains (just launched first brand TV/Cinema campaign this month), Epsom (just launched pan European TV and print campaign) and Childline.

'Also over the four years I have worked on many of the agency's other clients – Nastro Azzuro Peroni Beer, Natural History Museum, Royal Horticultural Society Shows, Hasbro, Amarula Cream Liqueur and Tio Pepe spring to mind.'

Stephen Brookes graduated in 2002 with first class honours in Communication Culture and Media. Since graduating he has become a journalist, researcher and public relations worker specialising in disability and diversity issues. He creates and contributes to various research projects as well as giving seminar presentations (including keynote speeches) on the issues facing disabled people in everyday life on disability issues.

He has worked with several local and national authorities and bodies on disability issues and best value reviews. He has served as a disability consultant to the Office of the Commissioner for Public Appointments, and headed a working sub-group of a steering committee chaired by Dame Rennie

Fritchie, focusing on media issues relating to disabled people and public bodies.

He is a member of SCOPE, Chair of Engage, and often works with the British Council of Disabled People. In support of his professional tasks Stephen is Chair of the National Union of Journalists Disabled Members Council and is also the Equalities and Disabilities Officer for the North West branch of the National Union of Journalists. He is a member of SKILL's Further Education/Higher Education council and generally works on issues facing disabled students.

Kelly-Anne Smith also graduated in 2002 and now presents the drive-time show on Virgin Radio. She explains what attracted her to a Communication Studies undergraduate programme, how she used her studies to pursue her career ambitions, and what she now does:

'I went to Cov. Uni, purely for the work experience on the CCM course. As it happened I loved the course, and learnt invaluable information from a host of excellent lecturers.

'The work experience, however, was vital to my career path. During my time at Coventry, I did work experience for local radio station, KiX96fm, in addition to setting up Phoenix student radio station as a permanent operation.

'During my second year I did every job going at KiX96fm, so that in my third year, I actually presented a paid Sunday show (so much better than working in a pub or a supermarket).

'Working this hard during my time at Coventry ensured that I walked straight into a presenting job when I finished my degree.

'I went on to present the breakfast show for KiX's sister station in Loughborough, and after only three months there I was taken on by 106 Century FM, which broadcasts to the East Midlands, and was a huge step up.

'I started reading the travel on Century, with a weekend show, and progressed to the evening show. I was at Century for 18 months, before Virgin Radio approached me to present their brand-new evening show.

'I came to Virgin in August 2003, and within five months, was promoted to their prestigious drive-time show.

'I wouldn't be where I was without the complete backing of the lecturers on the CCM course.

'I graduated with first class honours, and am now presenting a drive-time show on a national radio station – I couldn't ask for more than that!'

One year after graduating in 2003 Michelle Wayland has her own newscast for NBC in San Diego, California. Another busy media worker she grabbed a few moments to talk about herself and her job:

'I'm going to be producing the 6 pm news on the weekend. I didn't have a clue what I wanted to do when I left, and I only got a 2.2, but here I am with a great career that I love at 24.'

Hayley Boyes graduated in 2004. She now teaches English in China:

'After finishing my degree I wanted to realise an ambition that I've had for many years, to visit an exciting and vibrant country, China.

'I applied to work for the British Council as a language assistant in a school, what they wanted from us was enthusiasm, dedication, the ability to be adaptable and of course some experience of teaching.

'After asking for advice from the excellent International Office at Coventry University I found out about the places and customs, and for some valuable advice and information to research.

'I am based in Nanjing, Jiangsu Province where I teach in a primary school.'

When they were Communication undergraduates all these students took core (compulsory) modules in Communication Studies, Media and Cultural Theory, Cultural Analysis, Group Media Project, Work Placement and Final Year Dissertation. The option modules they took were Advertising,

Communication Practice, Journalism, Photography & Digital Imaging, Popular Music, and Video & Moving Image Production. So you can see how they synthesised theoretical and practical perspectives to prepare themselves for work in the communication, information and media industries.

4 MAPPING THE FIELD

This chapter is designed to give you a map outlining the main areas of human activity to which Communication Studies may be applied. Viewed one way it represents a journey outwards from communication on the smallest level to communication which takes place on a large scale. We will start by looking at communication which takes place within the self, communication between pairs of people, and then communication within groups. We will then move on to look at how people communicate using non-verbal signs and systems, and then progress to verbal communication. After that we will examine those visual and graphic means of communication which human beings use. Expanding from simple and small groups we will move on to an analysis of communication in progressively larger social forms – in organisations, in society, in mass communication, in global communication and in public and political communication. Lastly, we will look at a key feature of contemporary communication, what is termed integrated communications, the coming together of diverse communication systems through human and other technologies.

FROM INTRAPERSONAL COMMUNICATION TO INTERPERSONAL COMMUNICATION TO GROUP COMMUNICATION

Human beings communicate with each other in ways that no other species does. We use language – the exchange of symbols or signs. This in turn leads us to think by using these symbols and signs. No other animal nor, so far as we are aware, anything else in the universe, does this. We uniquely have communication, not only with others, but also with ourselves. We are able to consider ourselves, to reflect on our own existence, to be, as the American social behaviourist George Herbert Mead puts it, the objects of our own awareness.

We often speak of 'talking to ourselves' or even, as Bob Dylan puts it in his song 'You're Gonna Make Me Lonesome When You Go', 'You're gonna make me give myself a good talking-to'. Much of our thinking is perhaps best characterised as a conversation with ourselves. Having language means that we are able to work out complex ideas and think through problems as if we were discussing them with someone else.

Now, it is important to stress that these internal conversations could only happen to someone who has conversations with others. As Ferdinand de Saussure (see **Semiotics**) points out, language is social. The German philosopher Ludwig Wittgenstein went to some lengths to demonstrate that there could be no such thing as a private language. To be able to think about yourself is to be a member of a community in which you can be spoken about by others.

This implies that the very sense of self – the very idea of our own existence – is possible only because we have a language in which we can refer to ourselves. At first this may strike you as a paradoxical idea, but when you think about it you may see that it makes sense.

When small children start to use language, they copy the way that adults speak. They refer to themselves as if they were other people – what grammarians call the use of the 'third person'. In other words, rather than saying 'I am holding the doll', an infant will say 'Jane is holding the doll'. The suggestion is that at this early stage, the child does not have a fully developed sense of her own identity, but rather is dependent on others' perceptions to understand her own existence. It is only when the child's use of language has developed to the point where she can say 'I' and 'me' that she is fully an object of her own thought. We know others because we know ourselves, and we know ourselves precisely because we see ourselves reflected by others.

Our first communication, then, is with others and only after that are we able to have inner dialogues.

One-to-one communication with others is, perhaps, the model for all human communication. The exchange of symbols between one person and another begins, for most of us, in the interaction with our parents, in most cases, principally with our mothers. From this we learn to communicate and exchange symbols, ideas and concepts with other people and so to take our place in human society.

However, communication is not restricted to that which we have with one other or with ourselves. Because language is a social activity and because humans are social animals, a great deal of our communication is with the group in which we find ourselves. To be a human communicator is to be a member of a society.

Thus Communication Studies looks at three levels of communication: that which we have internally with ourselves when we think in words; that which takes place between two people; and that which takes place between an individual and the collective.

NON-VERBAL COMMUNICATION

There's a very old joke that goes: Two psychologists are walking down the street when one turns to the other and says, 'You're fine, how am I?' The joke is based on the suspicion some psychologists have of words; actions, they believe, speak louder about how people feel, about what they're thinking, about how they're reacting. That suspicion and those beliefs inform a larger study of human behaviour – things we do that achieve meaning even when we are not speaking or writing. In fact, a very large part of our communication repertoire is not expressed in words at all.

Non-verbal communication (NVC) covers a wide range of activities and behaviours, by no means all of them conscious or deliberate. Not all researchers into non-verbal communication agree about what name to give this feature

of human behaviour, some preferring non-verbal communication and others preferring non-verbal behaviour. The
differences in nomenclature are not mere pedantry. They
signify the unease that some researchers feel about the
assumptions some people make about certain aspects of
non-verbal activity, not the least being that it is a communication system as finely tuned and articulated as a spoken or
written language.

A standard list of NVC would include posture, eye contact,
closeness to other people (proximity), whether you touch
them (and where), the way you dress, gestures, tone of voice
when you speak (paralanguage), and so on. Much of this
activity is popularly referred to as 'body language', but this is
misleading as it places too much emphasis on physical behaviour. It is further misleading because it assumes that NVC is a
language susceptible to semantic analysis (working out the
exact relationship between signs and their meanings). Even
within a single culture one single act of NVC will not necessarily have consistent meaning in every situation in which it is
used and in every single person's use of that behaviour.

Some aspects of NVC are almost, if not completely, univer-
sal for human beings. One example is the act of raising the
eyebrows when we catch the eye of someone we know or
recognise (watch people passing each other on the street or
corridor). However, most forms of NVC are culturally condi-
tioned. Therefore, when making judgements about NVC it is
most important to ensure that you are sensitive to the cultural
origins of the person you are observing. For example, people
from some cultures are much happier about being physically
close than others. In general, people from the town will be
used to having less 'personal space' around them than people
from the countryside. Similarly, people brought up in a
Mediterranean culture will be used to much closer contact
than people from Scandinavia. Someone used to a small personal space will tend to move towards the person they are
talking to. If that person has a large personal space they will
feel this to be intrusive and will be likely to step back. If they
are not sensitive to each other's sense of personal space they

will interpret the other as, respectively, unpleasantly intimate or cold and stand-offish.

A similar case arises with eye contact. In European and American cultures, we tend to regard steady eye contact as a sign of honesty and reliability. Someone who is always looking away appears 'shifty' to us. Yet in many cultures direct eye contact is interpreted as challenging and confrontational; so what we see as suspicious may simply be someone else's way of being polite. This is before we factor in the degree of control which someone might exert over their non-verbal communication. If you live in a culture that assumes that 'the eyes are the windows on the soul' and that liars are unable to look you straight in the eye, an experienced liar will make a point of looking you straight in the eye. (For a masterclass in this learned, performed behaviour watch any film about con artists (confidence tricksters) such as David Mamet's *House of Games* or Steven Soderbergh's *Ocean's Eleven* where the con artists consistently play on unsuspecting people's belief in this yardstick of truth.) Sigmund Freud observed that liars, however much they control their eyes and fix their gaze on their listeners' eyes, nevertheless cannot control their fingertips. Of course, this can in turn become another behaviour that the purposeful and professional liar can and will control.

Gestures are another instance of potential cultural misinterpretation. The thumbs up gesture, for example, is used throughout most of the world to signify 'OK' or 'good' but in some parts of south-eastern Europe, such as Turkey, it means something very rude indeed.

One area of non-verbal communication that has great significance in most cultures is appearance. The clothes we wear, the way we groom our hair, the way we use make-up, jewellery, the way we adorn ourselves, all convey a great deal of information. Sometimes this is very obvious, for example in the wearing of uniforms by the armed services or the police. Sometimes the codes are less precisely laid down but it is still easy to see when someone is breaking them. For example, business dress for men in British culture typically consists of a suit, a shirt and a tie. (The rules for women are slightly less clear, although they are also clearly based on creating and maintaining a conservative image.) Someone like Sir Richard Branson, a successful businessman who deliberately flouts traditional British dress code, sends out lots of powerful messages about his status ('I can break the rules because I am important'), his independence, his freedom of spirit, and his wealth (being rich means never having to play by the rules). A powerful statement of this kind was made by Gordon Brown when, on becoming Chancellor of the Exchequer in 1997, he refused to wear formal evening dress (dinner jacket and white bow-tie) to formal functions and turned up at the Mansion House dinner in lounge suit and tie.

Sometimes the codes are understood only by people within a particular group. This is often the case with youth subcultures where a particular brand or style of clothing may have significance to other members of the group or to members of another group which people of their parents' generation entirely fail to notice or cannot understand. This sometimes occurs because a particular youth subculture takes an item of clothing from their grandparents' clothing repertoire and inverts its meaning. In the way in which we earlier voiced our unease about reading non-verbal behaviour as a precise language, older generations frequently read clothing aspects of non-verbal communication in a spectacularly incorrect way: for example, British politicians warning voters that all young people dressed in caps and hooded sweatshirts are delinquents ('Wearing baseball caps and hoodies – lock 'em up').

There are even non-verbal aspects to verbal communication. When we speak we give out a lot more information than that which is conveyed by the words themselves. Our tone of voice (calm, measured, tense, angry, cautious, confident, fearful) tells the listener a great deal about us. So does our accent. Typically, in any culture, accent is a marker of the place you come from. In Britain most people would instantly identify a speaker as coming from London, Liverpool or Belfast, just as most Americans would easily tell who came from New York, Houston or San Francisco. However, while most Britons would be able to tell someone was American and most Americans would spot a Brit, the finer gradations might be much harder for us to work out.

Accent is also a marker of social class. As Professor Higgins says in George Bernard Shaw's play *Pygmalion* (and the musical based on it, *My Fair Lady*), as soon as one Englishman opens his mouth, another Englishman despises him. The Inshman Shaw's point was that English culture is particularly snobbish about accent, but in fact regional and class distinction based on accent, is a widespread phenomenon throughout the world.

Non-verbal communication is not always deliberate or even conscious. Sometimes a person's way of speaking or posture will show us that they are nervous or even make us think they are trying to deceive us. In such an instance we would feel that their NVC was giving away something they were trying to conceal. Equally, some NVC can work without the receiver of the information being consciously aware of what is happening, as with the subtle deployment of perfume.

If you want to find out more about non-verbal communication a light treatment of the subject can be found in Allan Pease's *Body Language: How to Read Others' Thoughts by Their Gestures* (1984). A standard work by one of the most eminent researchers into non-verbal communication is Michael Argyle's *Bodily Communication* (1988). While non-verbal behaviour is a standard feature of the 'A' level Communication Studies specification and of long-established Communication degrees, nowadays it is just as likely to be studied in the context of a degree or modules in Social Psychology or in one of the hybrid Communication courses we looked at in chapter 3. In addition, the insights possibly afforded by the study of NVC often prove useful in the study of public and political communication.

VERBAL COMMUNICATION

The most basic situation in which verbal communication takes place is face-to-face communication. Within Communication

Studies this is more often termed dyadic communication. Common examples of dyadic communication are two people speaking with each other face-to-face, two people bumping into each other in the corridor, two people speaking with each other over lunch, or two people speaking on the telephone. Dyadic communication involves people using more than the one channel to communicate with each other.

Two people facing each other will communicate in the following ways: the clothes they wear (clothing semiology); the postures they adopt with their bodies (kinesics); the tone of voice they adopt when speaking (paralanguage), and so on. In other words, there is a terrific amount of information batting back and forth between these two people. At the very least we can categorise this information as facts, feelings, opinions and beliefs. So one person could ask another, 'What time does the Contemporary Cultural Theory lecture start?' or 'Do you know who Gill is who's booked the video edit suite all afternoon?' If the answer to the first question is 'eleven o'clock', then we would be dealing with facts. If the answer to the second question is 'that stupid cow Kylie', we would be dealing with feelings. If the response to the second question was 'Those stupid technicians need to install a proper booking system that doesn't let things like that happen', then we have moved to the voicing of opinion. And if the response led to someone saying, 'The problem with this university is that no one ever takes responsibility for systems – and no one cares about making sure all students have equal access to equipment', then we have moved further still – to the area of belief. Communication here will be achieved not only by what the two people say but also by how they say it. In the examples of the responses we gave, an expression of despair, disgust or anger on one of the speaker's faces will convey as much as the actual words spoken. It is highly likely that these two people are able to communicate with each other so richly because of such factors as shared feelings, shared beliefs and shared opinions, as well as sharing dress styles, if not belonging to the same culture or subculture. Obviously with verbal communication over the telephone much of the information transfer, exchange or sharing is achieved by non-verbal behaviour. And so in this situation paralinguistic features such as stress, intonation, pauses, emphases will all help the speakers' communication.

Verbal communication becomes more complex as the number of people involved becomes greater. Where eye contact or any other form of personal contact is still possible then we classify this as small group communication. Examples of this form of small group communication occur within families, in social life and at work. In these situations verbal communication is important but it is supplemented by non-verbal features such as eye contact, eye movement, bodily posture, arm and hand gestures, facial expression and vocal intonation. The small group is also likely to be linked by a number of common or shared feelings, experiences or beliefs, not to say shared goals such as would happen with a work or task group. Unless there is a serious personality clash, in small groups communication is easy and fluent and is supported by other communication means and methods. The existence of many commonalities within a small group not only makes communication easier but also means that there is a wider agenda of topics for discussion and a wider range of achievable goals.

When a group reaches a size such that all members cannot make or maintain eye contact with each other, then we have a large group. This could take the form of a year-group meeting of undergraduate students. Many large-group situations are not democratic, that is to say there will be key actors identified as leading speakers and contributors to the meeting. In addition, seating arrangements or seating patterns frequently act against the democratic principle and locate some people in superior and some in subordinate positions. However hard the convenor of the meeting (a year tutor) tries to work against this by moving chairs into a circle or horseshoe pattern, it will still be the case that the agenda of communication possibilities in such a situation represents a reduction from those achievable in a small group situation.

By the time the number of people assembled for a meeting constitutes a crowd then most of the factors that make for easy and effective communication in small or large groups have disappeared from the scene. You find crowds at a football stadium, a music concert or at the national conference of a trade union. With such assemblies the actors present are clearly divided into key actors and audience. In other words, a superior/subordinate situation definitely exists. The key actors will speak or perform, often from a stage or dais, in a physically superior position to their audience. They will function as transmitters, in very much the situation Shannon and Weaver characterised as the communication process. The extent to which feedback can or would practicably be sought will be limited. The extent to which the audience can offer feedback will also be limited: they may cheer or boo, they may shuffle their feet to signify boredom or dissatisfaction, or they may vote with their feet and leave the stadium or the concert hall or arena. Their communication vocabulary is distinctly limited.

There are some very real opportunities to apply classic Communication theory to verbal communication. In early Communication theory redundancy was the name given to describe the way in which the content of any communication is predictable. Redundant information is not new. So if a speaker uses certain verbal behaviour patterns regularly or takes every opportunity to recapitulate ideas or information previously presented, then this will be an example of redundancy in communication. As such it is unlikely to be threatening or confusing to listeners.

The opposite of redundancy is entropy. Any content of any communication which is new or eminently unpredictable is described as being entropic. Entropy is generated by those parts of a communication which are new to listeners.

Like many terms in Communication Studies entropy is derived from other disciples – physics, mathematics and statistical thermodynamics. In those fields entropy is something which cannot be precisely calculated; rather, its properties can only be calculated only in terms of probability. What we are presented with in both statistical thermodynamics and statistical communication theory is an attempt to calculate what are the statistical probabilities of a state or of a source. As Colin Cherry explained it:

> In both cases we have an ensemble – in the case of gas an enormous collection of particles, the states of which (i.e. the energies) are distributed according to some probability function; in the communication problem, a collection of messages, or states of a source, again described by a probability function. (Cherry 1996: 215)

Thus in a communication situation an entropic state consists in maximum unpredictability where the predictable number of choices of messages are at a maximum. The aim of the effective communicator should be to reduce entropy and increase negative entropy, where the unpredictable number of choices is reduced to a predictable number of choices. In this sense the effective verbal communicator's project is that of minimising entropy and maximising redundancy.

Verbal communication is a key component in modules on Communication Studies programmes such as Broadcast Journalism, Public Relations, Communication Practice and any other module where public speaking or speaking to camera or microphone is involved. The study of verbal communication in the belief that it can be controlled and refined to achieve strategic gaols is a fundamental notion in Communication Skills and in those Communication Studies degree programmes where students are trained for work in the communication, cultural, information or media industries. As an object of theoretical study it is more within the domain of Discourse Analysis (or, as it is more commonly termed, within Communication Studies Critical Discourse Analysis).

VISUAL AND GRAPHIC COMMUNICATION

In the Communication Studies Toolkit (chapter 5 of this book) we will describe the theories of signs proposed by Ferdinand de Saussure, C. S. Peirce and Roland Barthes (see **Semiotics**). These can be applied just as much to nonverbal communication as to verbal communication. People use a wide range of signs and symbols in their interactions with the world and with each other. Because many of these signs and symbols are understood across a number of language communities it is tempting to think of them as being in some way 'natural', to think that they are understood by everyone without having to be learned because they 'look like' the things they represent (in Peirce's trichotomy they are *icons*). The conventional 'stick figures' used to identify men's and women's toilets are understood through most of the world, but a moment's thought will enable you to dismiss the notion of the 'naturalness' of such signs.

Men and women don't really look like that. Many women, even in Europe and America, don't wear skirts. In many cultures, such as the great majority of the Islamic world, women never wear skirts. What's more, even if you can make the leap necessary to connect these signs with men and women, how do they come to represent toilets? Male and female symbols could just as easily have been used:

Here there is no suggestion that the symbols 'look like' the things they are taken to represent. They have meaning only because we agree to the convention that they do. In Peirce's trichotomy of signs they are *symbols*.

Another example is the control symbols on electronic recording and playback devices such as tape, CD, or DVD players and recorders.

Anyone familiar with using these machines will have no difficulty in identifying these as 'play', 'fast forward', 'rewind', 'stop' and 'pause'. But in order to do so we had to learn to read them in this way. The earliest machines had to have the actual words 'PLAY', 'EJECT', 'FAST FORWARD', 'REWIND', 'STOP' and 'PAUSE' written on the controls. Only when use of the machines had increased and people had become familiar with the controls did the use of symbols become possible.

We are surrounded by signs and symbols of all kinds: road signs, shop displays, advertisements and graffiti, to name but a few. Some, like road signs, are designed to be very clear and specific (otherwise driving would be very dangerous). Others, like graffiti, may be cryptic and wilfully obscure, designed as much to keep people out of communication as in communication. However, all of them carry and generate meaning.

But not all signs are intentional or deliberate. For example, a detective may discover traces of gunpowder in a room and conclude that this is where the shot was fired from. In that case the gunpowder is a sign of the shooting (in Peirce's trichotomy it is an *index*) but it is hardly intended to be a communication between the gunman and the detective.

In this sense everything around us is a sign. What we casually refer to as the 'built environment' – the buildings, the streets and other human constructions around us – obviously carries clear traces of human activity. An architect's design, a mason's mark, an advertising hoarding a set of traffic lights are obvious and intentional acts of communication. What is surprising is the extent to which this applies to the whole of our environment.

We conventionally think of cities and towns as 'artificial' and of the countryside as 'natural', but this is a false notion. Fields, hedgerows and woods have all been planted by people. Everything about the countryside bears the trace of human activity every bit as much as the streets and buildings of big cities. Indeed, because we are compulsive generators of meaning, we will read signs even in places where no human being has ever been, sometimes correctly as when sailors read the sun and stars to determine their position, sometimes incorrectly as when the lines of the surface of the planet Mars were believed to be canals and thus indexes of intelligent life.

Even outer space bears traces of human activity in the form of radio signals we have been generating for more than a hundred years and which radiate from this planet at the speed of light. And, if the theory of global warming is correct, even the weather is a human artefact.

This understanding that everything around us carries meaning, that we can read all of our surroundings as a text, was summed up by Karl Marx when he asserted, 'men can see nothing around them that is not of their own image; everything speaks to them of themselves. Their landscape is alive'.

ORGANISATIONAL COMMUNICATION

Communications have always been the key to the effectiveness of any human activities that involve the co-operation of a number of people. This is true of a wide range of endeavour, including politics, families, wars, agriculture, commerce, manufacture and warfare.

These days people are increasingly employed in industries which process information rather than making and handling material goods and objects. Communication itself is at the centre of our economic activity. Thus, for organisations, communication in various forms is more important than ever and the way in which companies communicate has become perhaps the most important factor in their success or failure. The body of knowledge that studies this is Corporate Communications.

Organisations have to manage communications in two directions. First, they must ensure that communication within the organisation is working well so that activities can be co-ordinated, instructions can be given, changes can be explained and information can flow from the operatives to the management to enable them to make effective decisions. This is internal organisational communication.

Secondly, organisations have to communicate with the world outside. Commercial companies have to deal with customers and suppliers. They have to tell potential customers about the products they are selling. They have to deal with governments and regulators and they have to manage the way they are seen by people outside the organisation. This is external corporate communication and includes advertising, sales and marketing, public relations, and news management and image management.

These basic communication needs are shared by all operations that involve getting a lot of people to work together. The balance of their importance may be different in some organisations from that in others, but all of them will have all of the requirements. For example, you might think that for an army, internal communication is highly important – the generals need to have good intelligence and to issue clear and effective orders. But their public image is also an important factor in their success. Troops who believe they are facing particularly brave, well-equipped or resourceful soldiers will be less inclined to stand their ground against them. The most powerful weapon of all that the British SAS or the US Navy SEALs possess is their reputation.

In politics, being able to affect and, if possible, control the way in which your candidate or party is portrayed publicly is essential. In some systems this is easier than in others. If the leader is an absolute monarch or dictator, they can force people to portray them in a certain way. For instance, the reason that most of the pictures we see of the English queen Elizabeth I look so similar is that they were all painted according to very strict guidelines and instructions from her court. In democracies, the task is more difficult. Much as they might perhaps wish otherwise, elected presidents and prime ministers cannot compel photographers, journalists or interviewers to portray them favourably. However, they can exercise a lot of influence.

SOCIETAL COMMUNICATION

Just as the idea of what society is has changed, and continues to change, so too has the idea of societal communication changed. All versions of history are just that – versions. They are stories we tell ourselves about ourselves to justify how we feel about ourselves, about other people, about our importance in the world in relation to other people, about how we arrived at the stage of 'evolution' or 'progress' we pride ourselves on having achieved. So in what follows here we are going to chart a history of societal communication which could very well be as partial as those story-tellings we have just warned you about.

In essence society before the modern age bore little resemblance to what we would now characterise as society. In feudal society populations were geographically spread out and, despite the fact that people were subject to the rule of feudal lords and kings, there was little sense of belonging to a larger community we would recognise in the term 'society'. What we now have no difficulty characterising as 'news' would often take the form of what we would now characterise as 'history': a medieval minstrel or wandering storyteller might take months to travel about England to tell people about, for example, the Battle of Agincourt.

It is possible to argue that it was the coming of mass communication that led to societal communication. While we look at the now problematic term 'mass communication' next we would argue that early forms of mass communication such as newspapers did assist in the creation of a shared public space in which people could come together to form a society; as the American playwright Arthur Miller has observed: 'A good newspaper is, I suppose, a nation talking to itself'. Of course, there are some caveats we must immediately enter here. Newspapers, like all other forms of mass communication, are owned by somebody, and they own newspapers in order to have influence, to have an effect (as Rupert Murdoch is rumoured to have said, 'I didn't come all this way not to have influence'). So whatever communication takes place within a newspaper and between the newspaper and its audiences will necessarily be shaped by this. In addition, mass communication in the early years of the twentieth century was less plentiful and more focused than it is now, so it did serve a unifying function.

Clearly, newspapers were overtaken by television in terms of audience size but, as with other forms of mass communication, television itself no longer performs a unifying function due to the proliferation of channels. Public events such as the coronation of Queen Elizabeth II in 1953 or the state funeral of Sir Winston Churchill in 1965 brought the UK to a standstill as British society crowded around television sets to watch. So it was once possible to conceive of society communicating with itself by virtue of the vast majority of people in a country doing the same thing at the same time. Elvis Presley's death, John Lennon's assassination and Kurt Cobain's suicide had progressively less impact on a social formation we could call society and, apart from the national outpouring of grief at the death and funeral of Princess Diana it's difficult to think of another event that unified society. (The reaction to 9/11 was not uniformly shock and sorrow.)

The history of the medieval world was one of city states small states, and large (geographically diverse) empires. As European countries emerged from their internal conflicts and revolutions of the sixteenth, seventeenth and eighteenth centuries we began to see the formation of what we would now recognise as the nation-state. Societal communication was vitally important for the nation-state in terms of how it thought about itself, about how it reinforced its sense of being a society and about how it interpreted events in line with its vision of itself. But now the apparently stable notion of the nation-state is beginning to unravel. This is happening for any number of reasons, not the least of which is the proliferation of nations: there are now more nations in the world than ever before: the United Nations in 2002 had 189 members compared with 51 in 1945. The nation-state is further destabilised by countries coming together to form larger economic or trading units or to form political alliances. It is also threatened by the emergence of a greater sense of regional pride. As Wally Olins has observed:

> the primacy of the nation-state is being questioned, from above by regional integration, from Mercosur in Latin America to NAFTA in North America and above all the European Union, and from below, as regionalism within Spain, Italy, Belgium, Canada, Britain and elsewhere is now joined by regionalism across nations, like the Danish-Swedish Oresund. In the United States many states are trying to assert themselves both politically and economically. In addition countries everywhere are removing themselves from many of their traditional roles in health, education, even security, and letting companies deliver these services instead. (Olins 2003: 158)

Whether viewed from the postmodern perspective of Jean Baudrillard (see **Postmodernism**) or from the free market position of Margaret Thatcher it is very difficult to think of society in the twenty-first century resembling society in the twentieth century. In December 1966 the BBC broadcast *Cathy Come Home* in a series of filmed plays called *The Wednesday Play*. The play told the story of a young family who experienced economic deprivation, became homeless and were then broken up by social workers and council officers. The play was watched by millions of people who were uniformly shocked and stunned by its vivid portrayal of a cruel reality. In addition, the broadcasting of the play is widely credited with the formation of Shelter, the campaigning and charitable organisation which speaks out for the homeless. This was an example of a society communicating with and about itself where a majority of the British people were watching the same programme on the same channel on the same day at exactly the same time (when there were only two terrestrial television channels and no cable or satellite television at all).

This is no longer possible. Today, many people would not see the programme because they didn't subscribe to the channel which broadcast the play. Or they would watch it, but would do so much later as they used their VCR or DVDR to time shift their viewing. Or the programme would be broadcast on a minority channel with very small viewing figures.

Combining the perspectives of marketing, which thinks of society in terms of niche audiences (and seeks to promote goods and products to niche markets), and that postmodernist tendency, which holds that society has so atomised that it is not possible to think of it in mass terms, we can see how a large-scale model of societal communication is inappropriate but a small-scale one is not. The same objects of communication can be simultaneously redundant and entropic when viewed by different audiences; and those communications can simultaneously create and reinforce both societal membership and exclusion.

Let's take a simple example from contemporary television. In the penultimate episode of season five of *The Sopranos* ('Long-Term Parking'), Christopher (Michael Imperioli) enters Tony's office. Tony (James Gandolfini) asks him, 'Where the fuck you been? You're late'. And Christopher replies, 'Highway was jammed with broken heroes on a last-chance power drive'. Bruce Springsteen fans would have recognised this as being a direct quotation of the first two lines of the fourth verse of his song 'Born to Run'. Thus it is possible to see how a smaller, less material, more virtual society emerges in their common interests and, in spotting the reference, they reinforce their sense of themselves as belonging to that society. (Indeed, many fans clubs actually call themselves societies.) To anyone outside that frame of reference this would sound obscure or unduly poetic; which is how

Tony heard it when he replied to Christopher, 'Oh, you're gonna get fuckin' cute now'.

MASS COMMUNICATION

Historically speaking one of the main aspects of mass communication studied in Communication Studies has been the effects it does or does not have on its audiences. 'Effects theory' is problematic as it is questionable whether exposure to mass communication media produces effects in terms of overt physical or verbal behaviour. On the one hand, if exposure to mass communication media does not produce effects, then the time, effort and money of business organisations, advertising agencies and political parties are being wasted. On the other hand, definite conclusions as to whether exposure to mass communication media has any effects have not been reached, not because insufficient research has been conducted into it but because the results of all those researches are either inconclusive or contradictory. The whole issue is further complicated by ideology: some people are ideologically predisposed to believe – absolutely – in mass communication media-producing effects, others are ideologically predisposed to believe that it produces no effects. This is often related to particular moral or political positions and to attempts to promote or oppose the censoring of certain films or popular songs or books or television programmes.

Let's look at some of the theorisations about how mass communication media might affect people.

The 1940 US presidential election was monitored closely in Erie County, Ohio, by Paul Lazarfeld. Together with a team of researchers he was trying to establish how voters were influenced in their voting behaviour. His researches suggested that mass communication media do not directly influence people but rather influence key people in social groups, what Lazarfeld termed opinion leaders or influentials, who in turn influence group members. When these researches were published in 1944 he stated, 'ideas often flow from radio and print to opinion leaders and from these to less active sections of the population'. The results of these researches were subjected to further analysis, and in 1955 Lazarfeld, together with Elihu Katz, published *Personal Influence* in which they presented their full-blown, two-step model of the way in which they believed mass communication media may influence personal opinion.

Until the time of their researches mass communication theory had conceived of mass communication media influencing isolated individuals who happened to be members of a mass audience. Katz and Lazarfeld presented their account of the process as being one where mass communication media influenced opinion leaders who subsequently influenced individuals who happened to be in social contact with those opinion leaders. Although received as a major contribution to media sociology at the time, the notion is at best hazy and imprecise as many subsequent contributors have pointed out. At best it might be profitable to think of the two-step flow of communication model as a useful sociological tool to understand social, family and work structures at the time. In 1940s America the power, influence and status of people such as fathers, priests, mayors, labour union leaders and politicians fitted their notion of opinion leaders. Interestingly enough, many influential people, particularly those who work in media and related industries, continue to think of people in terms of opinion leaders or opinion formers. So just because a theory about mass communication has been discredited it doesn't mean that some people cease believing in it.

To pose the question of media effects or media influence in this way begs one important question: why is it that some people modify their behaviour in response to mass communication messages and some do not? Even the criticism levelled at Katz and Lazarfeld's model – that people are not fixed in their roles as opinion leaders and opinion followers – fails to address itself to the fact that some people do not respond on some occasions to the messages of mass communication. This could be because research has tended, historically speaking, to look at the power of mass communication messages rather than at the psychological makeup of the target audiences of mass communication messages (or because the audience hasn't been appropriately theorised or because of the reductionist character of these audience theorisations). It could also be because a basic psychological model has been assumed about the process by which people learn new behaviours. This runs like this:

where it is assumed that a stimulus (in the form of a message) is made to an organism (a person, an audience member, a receiver) and a response (an effect) is produced.

But the world is full of examples of this process quite plainly not working. In the UK in 1960 the manufacturers of Strand cigarettes made a profound and powerful appeal to smokers in their advertising campaign: 'You're never alone with a Strand'. Despite the power of this appeal smokers failed to respond and maintained their loyalty to their existing brand of cigarettes. It might have been that smokers failed to relate to the lone figure in a white mac on the London Embankment, but this is difficult to prove. What cannot be doubted is that the Strand campaign featured an advertising slogan that was psychologically astute but economically disastrous.

People also exhibit a remarkable capacity not to see or hear what is being communicated to them. In 1960s America industries grew up committed to achieving behavioural change in people. Concerns about juvenile delinquency and racism led to active research being conducted: if behaviour was to be changed, there had to be an understanding of how it had come about. Researchers at Harvard University conducted one piece of research where they exposed research subjects to images and asked them questions. One such image was of a group of people on a subway train. In the middle of the picture are two men: a taller black man with his hands pointing down and a shorter white man with an open razor in his hand. The research subjects were asked to say who had the razor in his hand. Half of the observers reported seeing the razor in the black man's hand. So although there was a clear visual message in the picture a considerable number of people failed to respond to the information and simply saw something in accordance with their prejudice. This research established that racist people fail to read what is before their eyes and simply see what they want to see.

So what is missing from this equation if the stimulus– organism–response model doesn't explain how people are influenced or how their behaviour is changed? Melvin DeFleur has suggested that individuals respond to persuasive messages not because of the intrinsic power of these messages but because of a predisposition in their psychological makeup. He suggests that when individuals are exposed to a persuasive message this may match the psychological processes within those individuals, which will in turn trigger a form of slightly modified behaviour in them. In other words, it is the psychological predisposition which sets in motion the behaviour of the individuals. This behaviour will be changed not in its content, that is radical change is unlikely, but rather in its expression. DeFleur's Psychodynamic model (1970) does not get right away from the stimulus–organism–response model but it does introduce more variables, and offers significant modifications to the elements present.

Later researches into the effects of mass communication have tended to follow the more relativistic line of inquiry opened up by DeFleur. Contemporary conclusions are much more modified, as in Klapper's famous pronouncement: 'Some kinds of communication of some kinds of issues, brought to the attention of some kinds of people under some kinds of conditions, have some kinds of effects'. In addition, for at least the last twenty-five years, Communication Studies researchers have tended to focus their attention on how audiences use mass communication. David Morley's studies of how families watched and used television programmes in Coventry (published as The 'Nationwide' Audience in 1980) was an early example of this line of inquiry. He felt that audiences were not passive receivers of television's messages but rather were active participants in the viewing process and put their viewing of television programmes to uses not intended by the programme makers. This sense in which the audience has moved from being adoring to being active is at the heart of many contemporary theorisations about mass communication in Communication Studies. This position also sits well with notions such as the Death of the Author and the end of Grand Narratives (see **Postmodernism**) where a focus on producers and products is replaced by a focus on audiences and reception. Of course, given the proliferation of traditional forms of mass communication (film, television, records, books, newspapers and magazines) and the explosion of forms of new media (mainly accessible through personal computers and portable communication devices) it quite possibly makes little sense to think of this form of communication as being in any way mass.

GLOBAL COMMUNICATION

In 1964 Marshall McLuhan published *Understanding Media: The Extensions of Man*. It was here that he advanced the thesis that successive waves of communication revolution were about to culminate in what he conceived of as an implosion of the world (or certainly the western world). His vision of a wired-up world led him to coin the term 'the global village' as a witty and succinct way of thinking about a world that was rapidly shrinking as a result of communication technologies. No longer would it be the case that people knew nothing of societies on the other side of the world, or of events that were happening thousands of miles away.

In an age of 24-hour news broadcasting it is difficult to put oneself in the position of people 150 years ago. The sheer speed of contemporary news media to respond to major events is simply staggering. (As is the supplementing of news broadcasting with ordinary people's own moving images; nowadays virtually no world event is not captured on the digital cameras of non-professionals.) Earlier we spoke about the time it would have taken people around England to learn about the Battle of Agincourt. By the late nineteenth century it still took a long time for news of major events to get from one side of a country to another or from one country to another. News of the assassination of President Lincoln in 1865 took twelve days to get from Washington to London. But when Krakatoa erupted it was not the same communication world. In the intervening period Samuel Morse had invented Morse Code, Julius Reuter had founded his news agency and the submarine telegraph had been developed. In that way the eruption of Krakatoa can be thought of as the first tragedy of the age of global communication.

A Lloyd's agent saw the flames bursting from out of the volcano. He sent a message reading 'Strong volcanic eruption, Krakatoa Island' which was transmitted through lines that were soon wrecked by the tsunami that followed the eruption (and which killed 36,000 people). Before this happened his message had got through to Batavia, the capital of Dutch East India. From Batavia it was transmitted under the sea to Singapore. At Singapore the message was amplified and then sent on to Madras. It travelled across Sri Lanka and India through receiving stations at Trincomalee, Colombo and Bombay. It passed to Port Said in Egypt by means of the recently dug Suez Canal. It then went via Malta and Gibraltar to Porthcurno in Cornwall. Finally, it sped to Reuters' receiving stations in Newfoundland and Boston. As a result of all these then new information and communication technologies coming together the *Boston Globe* had the story on its front page four hours after Krakatoa erupted (Winchester 2005).

The integration of information and communication technologies came about not because of the public's voracious reading habits but because entrepreneurs found they could make money through the facilitation of faster communication. None of the business people involved here did what they did through the kindness of their hearts; they did it because there was money to be made. So the story of global communication is also the story of the advancement of capital.

In that sense it is very difficult to think about global communication without thinking about processes of globalisation. Depending on where one stands in the ideological spectrum dictates how one feels about globalisation. Those people who welcome change and who believe in the seventeenth-century notion of 'progress' tend to welcome it as they believe it is part of a process of making the world smaller and therefore friendlier (and more open to international trade). Those people who are more culturally conservative, not to say pessimistic, tend to believe that globalisation is part of a process of imperialism carried on under a different name, that it consists in the exporting of western ills to what are condescendingly termed 'the developing world'. In terms of media products it is very difficult not to think of globalisation as an extension of cultural imperialism. Virtually wherever you finds yourself in the world where there is television (and it's difficult to find parts of the world where there isn't television) you will find you recognise the programmes being broadcast even if you don't understand the language (and there's a strong likelihood you will understand the language as it could well be English). This is because whole television programme formats such as *Ready Steady Cook* or *Do You Really Want to be a Millionaire?* have been exported unchanged to all parts of the world. Add to that the selling of programme formats that are slightly modified (not every television channel in the world calls the programmes *You've Been Framed* or *Hollywood Squares*) and the copying of, for example, the formats for news broadcasting (in terms of presentation conventions, studio and news presenters' colour schemes, presenters' mannerisms, and sequencing of news items ('And finally . . .')) and you have a compelling argument for the cultural imperialism thesis. Next time you find yourself in a holiday hotel room and you turn on the television think about this.

PUBLIC AND POLITICAL COMMUNICATION

Governments, perhaps more than any other form of organisation, have to be able to communicate effectively with the people they govern. There is little use in passing a new law if no one knows about it. Thus a proclamation must be issued. In medieval times, kings would send messengers to tell the people what the king's instructions were. In today's world governments are able to communicate much more speedily and effectively through the mass media.

Another change since the Middle Ages has been the rise of democracy. This has made the effective use of communication by politicians still more important to them. Now they have to communicate, not merely instructions or orders, but explanations, justifications and reasons. Retaining power in a democracy means retaining the consent of the governed so our leaders, unlike medieval monarchs, have not only to tell us what to do but also to convince us that we should do so. They also need us to communicate with them so that they know what is or isn't acceptable to us, the people.

Politicians also seek to influence the way that the people think about things, to alter public opinion. This is the function of propaganda. The word 'propaganda' these days has a rather menacing implication because of its association with totalitarian regimes, although it originally meant telling the truth to people – spreading the word. In the twentieth century it is perhaps most closely associated with the regime of Nazi Germany under Hitler's Minister of Propaganda, Josef Goebbels. Communist regimes were also heavily dependent on propaganda agencies. The work of propaganda in totalitarian societies is satirised by George Orwell in his novel *1984*.

However, it is not only openly totalitarian regimes that set out to manipulate. Noam Chomsky and Ed Herman's *Manufacturing Consent* details the ways in which the 'western democracies' use techniques derived from public relations and advertising to control and manipulate public opinion. They go so far as to suggest that this is so effective and widespread that it undermines the very notion of democracy and calls into question the legitimacy of these governments.

The flow of information has always needed to be two-way. To govern a state, a nation or a people requires detailed knowledge about them. Governments obtain this through censuses, surveys, the maintenance of large banks of data, such as the social security system, health records or the Driver and Vehicle Licensing Centre, and opinion polls. Much of this information is collected and analysed numerically in the form of statistics. In fact, the very word 'statistics' comes from the same root as the word 'state'.

In recent years in Britain, all political parties, but particularly the 'rebranded' New Labour of Tony Blair, have been accused of governing through the excessive use of such techniques to manipulate news coverage, to mislead the public and to obtain consent that would rationally have been withheld. While it is undoubtedly true that the 'spin doctors' of New Labour, particularly Alastair Campbell and Peter Mandelson, have been exceptionally effective on many occasions, there is nothing new or unusual about governments, parties and leaders using every technique available to them to ensure that they present the case as favourably as possible to themselves. It would be naive in the extreme to expect anything else.

INTEGRATED COMMUNICATIONS

One of the key concepts in the study of communication over the last quarter of the twentieth century has been convergence. Whereas at one time the technologies of communication (television, newspapers, telephones, film, radio) all seemed quite distinct, since the arrival of microprocessor technology (the microchip) in the 1970s there has been a steady process of the coming together of these technologies with each other and with the new technologies only made possible by the new electronics – computers, the Internet, mobile telephones, digital cameras and small, portable, high-volume data storage devices like iPods.

This convergence of the 'hardware' has been paralleled by similar developments in the communicative behaviour of people using these devices. Increasingly, this is leading to a new type of communications profession in which people need to have a much broader range of skills and knowledge.

Corporate communications, for example, used to be compartmentalised into a number of discrete areas or disciplines such as Internal Communications, Public Relations, Advertising, Communication Management, Shareholder Reporting, Marketing, Market Research and Corporate Image Management. Obviously, from time to time these functions and roles overlapped (or, if the organisation was unlucky, they clashed). As communication has become recognised as a more high-profile activity than it used to be regarded, organisations have begun to realise that they need to take a more consistent approach.

Because people in general have so much more access to information, an organisation can no longer assume that the content of the shareholder report can stand entirely apart from advertising or news management. Inconsistencies between public statements by an organisation in different forums will be quickly exposed and publicised in the mass media.

An awareness has, therefore, grown of the desirability of linking all the organisation's communication functions together. Many organisations do this in-house, but there has also been a trend in the communications industries for agencies to offer a one-stop shop for corporate communications so that they will offer services in advertising, public relations, internal communications and marketing, all in a single package.

5 THE COMMUNICATION STUDIES TOOLKIT

This chapter gives a brief introduction to a number of perspectives from which communication can be studied and the major theorists associated with these perspectives. They are:

- Semiotics
- Discourse Analysis
- Social Constructionism
- Visual Rhetorics
- Historical Materialism
- Psychoanalysis
- Gender Criticism (including Feminism, Postfeminism and Queer Theory)
- Structuralism and Poststructuralism
- Postmodernism
- Postcolonialism

This list is by no means intended to be exhaustive – there are many more perspectives from which theorists have analysed communication. No one approach is more or less valid than another. What matters is whether it reveals some insight into the text under investigation. Thus the fact that, for example, liberal humanist, ecological or market economic perspectives are not covered here in no way implies that somehow they have less authority than these. We simply had to restrict the list because of the space available. That said, looking at Communication Studies in an historical context there is a remarkable degree of consensus about who are and have been the thinkers who have shaped contemporary thought and what are the principal tools most appropriate to the investigation of the world. Mark Fortier has succinctly characterised those key thinkers who have shaped our times: 'Our own theoretical era, broadly conceived, began in the nineteenth century with G. W. F. Hegel, Karl Marx and Friedrich Nietzsche, continued into the early twentieth century with Sigmund Freud and Ferdinand de Saussure, and then into the middle of the century with, among others, Mikhail Bakhtin, Antonio Gramsci, Walter Benjamin and Simone de Beauvoir' (Fortier 1997: 2). And he has characterised the key tools used to analyse our times: 'Deconstruction, feminism, postcolonialism, semiotics, Queer Theory, postmodernism, and so forth, have come to define for many the most fruitful and appropriate ways of looking at culture, politics, and society' (Fortier 1997: 2). We could add that any student following an undergraduate programme in arts, humanities or social sciences at a British university will encounter at least half of the perspectives in our list of ten.

At the end of each of these ten introductions we offer some ideas and/or activities which will help consolidate your learning. This might take the form of simply restating who we think are the key writers on the subject, or advice about a key text a key writer has produced, or the address for a website which offers sound information for someone just starting to learn about the topic.

SEMIOTICS

Semiotics (sometimes also called semiology) is the science or study of signs. It has an interesting history, having been invented twice, quite independently, in Switzerland and in the United States. The Swiss linguist Ferdinand de Saussure coined the term 'semiology' when teaching about general linguistics. The American philosopher Charles Peirce, thinking about the logic of science, devised the term 'semiotics'.

When de Saussure was employed as a lecturer at the University of Geneva, he specialised and researched in the ancient language of Sanskrit, but as a condition of his appointment he also had to teach a course on general linguistics. Today his fame rests on a book published after his death and based on notes taken by students at the lectures from that course. Curiously, it appears that de Saussure himself did not realise the significance of his discoveries in this field.

The *Course in General Linguistics*, published in 1916, revolutionised they way we understand not only language but all objects of human knowledge. It proposes a theory of the way that signs, such as words, convey meaning. The central concept of the theory is that signs are *arbitrary*, by which he means that words have their meanings only because we choose that they should. As Humpty Dumpty says in *Alice Through the Looking Glass*, 'When I use a word, it means just what I want it to mean – neither more nor less'. Language works, not as a function of 'human nature', but as a consequence of convention.

De Saussure defined signs as comprising two parts, the *signifier* and the *signified*. The signifier is the sound we make in speaking a word or the marks on paper or on a screen we use when reading or writing. The signified is the idea of what they represent. Thus the sound of the word 'tree' or the written or printed word is the signifier and the idea of a tree in your mind when you hear or read it is the signified.

De Saussure's point is that we could just as easily have used a different word. The word 'tree' is not linked to actual or even imagined trees by anything other than our agreement that it is. We could just as easily call a tree a 'klong' and so long as we all did so, we could still talk about the same objects. In other languages a tree is called something different ('arbre' in French, 'baum' in German, etc.). Indeed, it's when we move from speaking and writing our first language to learning how to speak and write a second language that we see how arbitrary the relation between signs and objects is.

(De Saussure also argued that we sometimes do use two words to refer to the same object within the one language. This is because, as he argued, we use our own first language at two levels: what he termed *langue* and *parole*. When we use our language in the way that most people in our culture do then we are using *langue*. This is how a language might be described by a grammarian or a bureaucrat – with all the local nuances ironed out. When we use language at a more personal level, for example within a family setting, or within a relationship, then we use a more allusive and less absolute form of language; this is *parole*. If nothing else, this is a very useful way of explaining how language difference occurs *within* a language.)

Nor is it only the signifier that is arbitrary. The signified, too, is a matter of convention. Not only is the choice of the word 'tree' rather than 'klong' a human decision, so too is the choice to have a single word or concept that encompasses a range of things, such as oaks, elms and palms, and excludes others, such as bushes and hedges. Whilst each actual tree is an object in the world, the idea of a tree is a human invention. It would be perfectly possible to have two different words – say, one for deciduous trees and one for evergreen trees – and to regard them as two quite distinct and discrete categories.

It follows from this that signs such as words can have meaning only because of the way they fit into a system such as a language. They are defined by contrast to what they are not. For example, cats are precisely not dogs, mice or people. The meaning of our words turns out not to rely on any correspondence between them and the material world but on their relationship to each other. A single sign, like the words 'boy', 'burning' or 'deck', has little significance by itself whereas, combined into a sequence with other signs, it becomes part of a dramatic image:

'The boy stood on the burning deck.'

These words are able to create this image because they are related to others within a system in two ways.

First, we could have chosen to use different words. Instead of 'boy' we could have written 'girl', 'captain', 'pirate', or a host of other things. Similarly, instead of 'burning' we could have written 'polished', 'upper' or 'flooded'. However, we cannot substitute any word; only certain words will make sense. For instance, we couldn't say 'the weather stood on the burning deck' The collection of words that can be substituted in this way for a particular word in a sentence is termed a *paradigm* and changes in meaning effected in this way are termed *paradigmatic* changes.

Secondly, there is the relationship between the words in the sentence. If we said, 'The deck stood on the burning boy' the sentence would still, in some sense, be grammatically correct and perhaps even meaningful to someone, but it would not have the same meaning. The order in which words are arranged is one of the things that establishes their meaning. The term we use to describe such a sequence is a *syntagm*. To change the meaning by changing the word order is to make a *syntagmatic* change.

Although rarely employed as a full-time university professor, Charles S. Peirce (pronounced 'purse') left thirty volumes of collected philosophical papers. Working in what we would now call an 'interdisciplinary' way, Peirce addressed many questions across a wide range of diverse disciplines. One of those questions centred on how people came to link words with things. Living and writing in the Boston area of Massachusetts he debated and argued with many key thinkers of nineteenth- and twentieth-century America. In *The Metaphysical Club* (2002) Louis Menand explains how Peirce worked through the problems about the relationship between words and things and in so doing most likely influenced other American thinkers of the time:

> There was no way to hook up ideas with things, Peirce thought, because ideas – mental representations – do not refer to things; they refer to other mental representations. When we hear the word 'tree', we do not perceive an actual tree; we perceive the conception of a tree that already exists in our minds. Peirce called this mediating representation an 'interpretant' (a term he introduced in 1866, in a lecture in Boston attended by [William] James and [Oliver] Wendell Holmes). (Menand 2002: 363)

The sign as conceived by de Saussure had two components: the signifier (the means by which we refer to objects) and the signified (the object itself). As we can now see, Peirce thought there was a third element: the interpretant. In Peirce's system the sign was composed of three elements: the sign (which corresponds to de Saussure's signifier), the object, the thing being referred to (which corresponds to de Saussure's signified) and the interpretant (or the mental concept of the object, as distinct from the sign). This three-part conception meant that Peirce's notion of the sign was a more active and dynamic one than de Saussure's. Accordingly, this concept of the sign could more easily be applied beyond spoken and written languages.

From this fundamental conception of the sign Peirce's thinking led him to think further about how signs actually function. He wasn't addressing the 'why?' or the 'what?' of communication, but rather the 'how?' To do so he invented a new word. Taking the existing word 'dichotomy' which means something which is divided into two, he devised the word 'trichotomy – meaning something which is divided into three. He argued that signs function in one of three ways: as icon, as index or as symbol. In all three cases the category of sign arises from the relationship between the object and the sign.

The character of the relationship between an iconic sign and its object is one of resemblance: an iconic sign looks like its object. Examples of iconic signs are photographs, videos and representational paintings.

The character of the relationship between the indexical sign and its object is one of existence, which is why an indexical sign is sometimes referred to as an existential sign. When we see an indexical sign we assume the existence of another sign. Examples of indexical signs are smoke, spots on a person's face or the moving hands of a watch or a clock. When we see smoke emerging from a chimney or from behind a hill we assume the existence of fire. When we see spots on someone's face we assume that they are an adolescent, or that they are ill, or that they have a poor diet. When we see hands moving on the face of a watch or a clock we assume the passing of time.

The character of the relationship between a symbolic sign and its object is arbitrary; that is, there is no logical or necessary connection but rather there is a social convention that has arisen over a period of time. Examples of symbolic signs are most spoken and written communication, non-representational painting and music. With all these examples we can make sense of the signs only because we have been introduced to conventions that link words and objects. Without that introduction we would be lost, as we are when we find ourselves in a country where we do not speak the language.

Apart from the students he taught few people knew of de Saussure's work in his lifetime; similarly, Peirce's work was little known in his lifetime. In both men's case we know of their work through their followers and their interpreters. Peirce was most unlucky in terms of how his posthumous reputation was achieved. Unread and unknown for a generation after his death Peirce's ideas only started to resurface in the 1950s via the works of C. W. Morris. Unfortunately, Morris adopted a very simple and reductive view of Peirce's work. Many of his unnecessary simplifications of Peirce's work survive to this day. (Don't be surprised if you witness a lecture where you are told that the character of the relationship between an indexical sign and its object is a causal one, that is, the one sign exists because the other exists. As you known from the previous paragraph, this is a distortion of Peirce's original, infinitely more subtle, explanation.) De Saussure fared rather better than Peirce. By 1915 his work had had a direct influence on Roman Jakobson and other linguists in the Moscow Linguistic Circle. When Jakobson moved to Prague and formed the Prague Linguistic Circle in 1926 de Saussure's influence spread even further. Jakobson eventually left Europe and moved to the United States, but de Saussure continued to influence European academic linguistic communities. And although de Saussure was only interested in spoken and written languages the fact that his ideas could be applied to other fields of activity quickly became apparent.

The insight that things have meaning according to how they are arranged within structure became the basis of the theory of structuralism (see **Structuralism and Poststructuralism**). For example, the anthropologist Claude Lévi-Strauss applied the same methods to the study of a range of human activity systems including families, mythologies and dinner-table etiquette to reveal that they all formed systems within which meaning was created by the relationship of one part to another.

De Saussure's ideas were taken up by Roland Barthes in the 1960s. Barthes was a cultural critic and one of the first people to apply semiotic theory to everyday objects and activities such as cars, steak and chips, wrestling and striptease. Between 1954 and 1956 he published monthly journalistic pieces where he took everyday objects and subjected them to semiological analysis. These pieces, or essays, were collected and published in a book called *Mythologies* (1957).

At the end of these essays, Barthes included a longer, theoretical essay explaining his development of de Saussure's notion of the signifier and signified. Barthes had realised that there are, in fact, two levels or orders of signification. The first-order, that described by de Saussure, and a second-order which is not about the words themselves but about the particular associations they have for the person reading writing, hearing or speaking them. De Saussure's theory emphasises the text, rather than the richness of meaning, and does not account for ambiguity and suggestion. What Barthes set out to do was to show how signs have different meanings for different people.

Barthes called the first-order of signification, the one described by de Saussure, denotation. Denotation is the process by which the common-sense, obvious, everyday meaning of the sign is created. A signifier and a signified together form the sign and this is used in a sequence of signs to produce meanings.

The second-order of signification Barthes identified he called connotation. At this level, the whole sign created in denotation becomes the signifier for a second round of meaning generation. The signified at this level is the context, both personal and cultural, in which the reader, listener or viewer of the sign understands and interprets it.

A good example of denotation and connotation is a photograph. Let us imagine a head and shoulders portrait.

The picture denotes the person photographed. However, the way in which the picture is taken, processed and presented will make a great difference to the way it is perceived. A black-and-white image with very harsh lighting and tight focus will convey a sense of strength and seriousness. A soft-focus colour image taken at the same time and from the same angle will appear much more gentle, relaxed, even romantic. Denotation is *what* is signified. Connotation is *how* it is signified. Think of the difference between a passport photograph and a fashion shot. One connotes actual or recognisable identity; the other connotes glamour, fame, desirability.

Connotation may work at a level shared across a whole culture – like the meanings we attribute to hard and soft focus – or may operate at a much more personal level. What may to one person simply be a picture of a man or woman, of a certain age and appearance, may to someone else be a parent, a lover, a leader or an enemy.

Connotation may be achieved through techniques, such as the framing, focus, aperture, camera angle, film stock and film speed used by a photographer or the tone of voice and speed of delivery of a speaker. It may also involve the use of cultural signifiers, for example when we depict a man in a bowler hat drinking tea to connote Englishness. In language, the choice of words can create huge differences in connotation. Think of sentences which might include either half of these pairs: 'action'/'war', 'invasion'/'liberation', 'forces loyal to the old regime'/'the resistance'.

Barthes contended that second-order signification creates myth. John Fiske (in his *Introduction to Communication Studies*) defines this as:

> a story by which a culture explains or understands some aspect of reality or nature. Primitive myths are about life and death, men and gods, good and evil. Our sophisticated myths are about masculinity and femininity, about the family, about the British policeman, about science.
>
> (Fiske 1990: 88)

Myths naturalise history, that is to say they make the results of human actions appear to us like works of nature – they make a state of things which is actually the result of human choices and actions seem inevitable. For example, until recently it was taken for granted by most people that gender roles were inborn, that men were breadwinners and women were nurturers. Really, this was just the result of the way in which society and culture had developed and not only is it possible to change things, but also a great deal of change has already been made within a couple of generations and is still going on.

Using semiotics to analyse and deconstruct these myths shows us their hidden history and political content and takes away the power of the myth to make unfairness seem inevitable.

Consolidation

The best place to start finding out about semiotics is this website:

http://www.aber.ac.uk/media/Documents/S4B/semiotic.html

Key names:

Roland Barthes – Try reading one or two of the short essays in Roland Barthes (1993) *Mythologies*, London: Vintage.

Or try this website: http://we.got.net/~tuttle/

or this one: http://orac.sund.ac.uk/~os0tmc/myth.htm

Ferdinand de Saussure – a good introduction is Jonathan Culler (1985) *Saussure*, London: Fontana.

Key ideas: signs, signification, signifier and signified, denotation and connotation

DISCOURSE ANALYSIS

'Discourse' literally refers to spoken language or, specifically, conversation. In the context of Communication Studies it means language in actual use, so Discourse Analysis is the study of actual instances of language use, particular things written or spoken, as opposed to the general rules or definitions that make up the language and make such specific instances of communication possible. In de Saussure's terms (see **Semiotics**) it is the study of acts of *parole*, as distinct from *langue*.

The essential idea underlying Discourse Analysis is that every act of communication is an action in the world. Each time we say or write something to someone, we are bringing about a change.

Again, like semiotics, the study of Discourse Analysis brings together strands of thinking from the English-speaking tradition of analytical or linguistic philosophy and the continental European one of poststructuralism.

In a famous series of lectures (published as *How to Do Things with Words*), the English philosopher of language, J. L. Austin, pointed out that in the model of language many people have, in which words stand for things and are linked together into utterances to make statements about those things, there are many uses of language which do not refer to something but are themselves actual actions. For example, when a judge says to a prisoner, 'I sentence you to five years' imprisonment', he is not saying that the prisoner will go to gaol, he is actually sending him there. His words are not a description of what will happen, they are in fact the action that makes them happen. Similarly, when a ship is launched, the words 'I name this ship the Queen Mary' are not used to say what the name is, they are the very action of giving the name to the ship. Austin called such statements 'performatives'.

Austin then went on to show that this is really the case with all statements. Every utterance actually brings about a change in the world when it is uttered. As a consequence, all statements, all uses of language, are performatives. This means that in order to understand what is going on when communication takes place, we must look at the effect that the communication has. In the paraphrased words of some of the followers of Austin's predecessor and supervisor, Ludwig Wittgenstein, 'Don't look for the meaning – look for the use.'

Following Austin there has been a great deal written about the philosophy of acts of communication and how they work.

This body of work is called 'speech act' theory and is still influential on the thinking of a great many thinkers and writers in the field.

The French philosopher Michel Foucault, working within a quite different intellectual tradition, was also interested in the ways in which acts of language use have effects in the world. In a series of books written throughout the 1960s and 1970s, he described the ways in which the language used to describe certain activities or conditions gave power over them to the person(s) using the language. He analysed the ways in which discussions of, for example, madness (*Madness and Civilisation*), criminality and justice (*Discipline and Punish*) or illness (*Birth of the Clinic*) are controlled by those in power within such contexts, because they control the ways in which they can be talked about. For example, the terminology and jargon of the psychiatric profession – talk of neurosis, psychosis, symptoms, treatment, medication, therapy and so on – means that madness is generally discussed in, and on, the terms of the medical profession, as 'mental illness'. This in turn gives doctors, and in particular psychiatrists, a privileged position in the discussion and denigrates the opinions of anyone else, including the 'mentally ill' themselves, as uninformed, or amateur.

Foucault suggests that knowledge always works in this way, to establish or reinforce a power relationship. For him, knowledge and power are indissolubly linked, so he talks of them as a single thing: knowledge/power (*savoir/pouvoir*).

A discourse analyst looks at any particular instance of communication in terms of the action that is taking place. She asks the question: 'When this is being said, what is being *done*?'

For instance, suppose you go for a job interview. When you go into the interview room, the chief interviewer greets you and invites you to sit down. She then says to her colleague, 'Mr Jones, would you close the window, please.' What is actually being done when she says this?

First, she is issuing an instruction. One effect of her action is to make Mr Jones close the window. At the same time she is demonstrating to you her status as the person in charge of the room; she has the authority to issue instructions. Of course, the action could fail. Mr Jones could reply 'Shut it yourself', in which case the action performed would be the unintended one of undermining the chief interviewer's authority.

Where Communication Studies offers one of its distinct features is the way in which it might combine the Discourse Analysis approach with elements of semiotics, psychoanalysis, power relations and gender relations, to produce a complex analysis. In this way the utterance 'Shut it yourself' could be further analysed in terms of the tone of voice used, the way particular words are stressed, the accompanying hand movements and so on, all of which could be shown to modify and refine the action's meaning.

Consolidation

A very comprehensive introduction to Discourse Analysis can be found at:
    http://bank.rug.ac.be/da/da.htm
Jonathon Potter and Margaret Wetherell wrote a comprehensive book on the use of discourse theory by psychologists which gives a thorough breakdown of their approach: Jonathon Potter and Margaret Wetherell (1987) *Discourse and Social Psychology: Beyond Attitudes and Behaviour*, London: Sage.
    You may find one of the following an easier introduction:
    Malcolm Coulthard (1985) *Introduction to Discourse Analysis*, London: Longman.
    Sarah Mills (1996) *Discourse*, London: Routledge.
    David Nunan (1993) *Introducing Discourse Analysis*, London: Longman.
    Key ideas: speech acts, rhetoric

SOCIAL CONSTRUCTIONISM

Many theorists have contended that, because we think in words and sentences, the world we see around us is, in fact, shaped by the language available to us to describe it. (To paraphrase the philosopher Ludwig Wittgenstein, the limits of my language are the limits of my world.) The American linguists Edwan Sapir and Benjamin Whorf, for example, famously proposed that because the Inuit people had a number of different words in their language for different kinds of snow, they actually perceived these as quite separate things, rather than as different types of the same thing. Similarly, they asserted that the Hopi, a Native American nation, had a quite different understanding of time from speakers of European languages. European languages, they claimed, contain words and concepts that predispose us to think of time in terms of beginnings, middles and ends. Our perception of time is linear, leading from past to future. For the Hopi, they said, time was circular. Their language constructs an understanding of time as one of recurrence and cycles (day and night, the seasons of the year), so that they see time as a continuing series of returnings.

There are a number of criticisms that can be made of the 'Sapir–Whorf hypothesis' as it is usually known (erroneously so, in the opinion of the present writers, since it is not susceptible to experimental testing), but there is not space in this volume to do them justice. It is widely held that a 'weak' version of it, which asserts that all our perceptions are affected by the language in which we describe them, is highly plausible but uncontroversial; however, a 'strong' version, asserting that all perception is entirely determined by language, is highly controversial and difficult to sustain.

The Sapir–Whorf position is, however, strongly supported by the work of Ludwig Wittgenstein. He argued strongly that the limits of our language are the limits of what it is possible to know. His first great book, *Tractatus Logico–Philosophicus*, ends with the admonition that those things of which we are unable to speak must be passed over in silence. In other words, there is no point in trying to understand or discuss those things for which we do not have language.

It is important to be clear that the writers and thinkers discussed here are not suggesting that the world exists only in language or ideas (a position technically termed, in philosophy, idealism). They are all committed to the real existence of the material world. What they assert is that our perception of that world is determined by our language and, although we can develop other perspectives by broadening our own language or learning others, we cannot get beyond language to make direct contact with the world. It is in this sense only that they contend that the world as we see it is a construction of our minds. Hence the term constructionism.

Another of Wittgenstein's points is that language is always a social activity – no one can develop a language of which she was the only speaker. Languages are by definition collaborative projects. That is why the position is called Social Constructionism.

It is not only the outside world that social constructionists claim is formed by the words available to us to describe it. The same is true of our inner perceptions, including our idea of our self.

The social psychologist George Herbert Mead developed the theory that the self comes into being as the infant learns those parts of language used for self-reference. In other words, we start to have a conception of self – as Mead puts it, we become objects of our own thought – at the time we become competent in the linguistic use of the first person, that is, when we can use the words 'I' and 'me'.

Social constructionism is closely allied to structuralism (see **Structuralism and Poststructuralism**) in that both propose that the distinction between two objects of thought is conventional or arbitrary, that is, it is a matter of human decision, rather than something outside us, in 'Nature'.

Consolidation

Try reading the introduction to Ken Gergen (1999) *Invitation to Social Construction*, London: Sage.

Or this:

Vivien Burr (1999) *An Introduction to Social Constructionism*, London: Routledge.

VISUAL RHETORICS

Rhetoric is the practice of using language to persuade. Traditionally, it was taught as a word-based activity, concentrating on public speaking. The origins of rhetoric are in political and legal debate and first flourished as a subject of study some two and a half thousand years ago in the republic of Athens. Classical Athens was a direct democracy in which all citizens took part in debate and voted on actions, rather as if all British adults were able to turn up for parliamentary debates. Of course it could only work because Athens was quite small and not everyone who lived there was a citizen – women, slaves and foreigners were excluded. The assembly functioned not only as a house of government, making laws and appointing officials, but also as a court of law, in which any citizen could bring a case against anyone. Since the assembly had the power to sentence people to death, a person's life could, quite literally, depend on their powers of persuasion. As a result, teachers of rhetoric could make a good living.

Throughout history, rhetoric has been looked at with some suspicion. It has always had a reputation of being about trickery or manipulation. We are distrustful of fast-talking salespeople, politicians or lawyers. As Ralph Waldo Emerson once observed of a public figure, 'The louder he talked of his honour the faster we counted our spoons' (*Conduct of Life*, 1870). We believe that people should speak simply, plainly and honestly, rather than setting out to use their words to produce a desired effect. This position is, of course, rather naive. Whenever we speak we are trying to persuade someone of something. There really is no such thing as 'plain speaking', but a distrust of professional communicators is as old as rhetoric itself. The philosopher Plato wrote an attack on the rhetorician Gorgias (first published in 380 BCE) in terms that we would recognise as being very much those used about today's advertising copywriters and political spin doctors.

A visual rhetoric, then, is an attempt to persuade or influence people by the use of images, rather than words. Of course, in many communications words and pictures are combined to achieve a greater effect. The most obvious place where we can see this going on is in advertisements. In a book called *Image, Music, Text* (1977) Roland Barthes analysed closely the way that imagery was used in a magazine advertisement for a brand of Italian food – pasta, tomato sauce, parmesan cheese, etc. He noted that the advertisement did not simply show a picture of the packets but depicted them spilling from a string bag, along with a couple of fresh onions. This gave the picture a sense of immediacy and freshness (even though all the food was packaged), as if someone had just rushed hungrily home from the shop to make spaghetti bolognese. He also noticed that the colours of the packaging reflected those of the Italian flag, giving the food an air of what he called 'Italianicity'. Without saying a word about it, the advertisement was telling us that the product was authentically Italian and, by implication, better than something packaged in a factory and shipped to supermarkets, although this was the reality. This sort of 'fake authenticity' was a phenomenon Barthes spent a lot of his time attacking and it is still evident in many advertisements today. Think of the Marlboro Cigarettes cowboy.

Persuasion takes place in venues other than advertisements, however, and may be all the more suspect because it is less obvious. After all, however clever and manipulative an advertisement may be, we are always aware that it is trying to persuade us and, as a result of this, we are frequently on our guard against getting sucked in by its rhetorical devices. When we uncover rhetorical devices in other forms of communication, we may find it more shocking.

Laura Mulvey, for instance, identified aspects of the way that films work to reinforce gender roles. Specifically, she pointed out that the film camera takes on characteristics of the way that men look at women. Her interpretation of the male gaze draws on the work of the psychoanalyst Sigmund Freud to make a case that the portrayal of women through this device reinforces their oppression. A similar point is made by John Berger in *Ways of Seeing* in relation, particularly, to paintings, especially nudes: 'Men look at women. Women watch themselves being looked at' (Berger 1972: 47).

Historically speaking advertising critique has been especially perceptive when inflected by feminist perspectives. One of the classic texts of early British Communication Studies is Judith Williamson's *Decoding Advertisements*. Kathy Myer's *Understains* is another classic text from this era. A quick and easy but most perceptive read is Janice Winship's 'Handling sex'. At one point in this essay she analyses an advertisement for an early domestic video cassette recorder. Her reading reveals the profound assumptions about gender implicit in even a supposedly innocuous advertisement. Although these works were first written and published over twenty years ago they continue to offer insights into reading the continuing influence of patriarchy as reproduced in advertisements, the wallpaper of our lives.

Consolidation

Although this book is based on a series of television programmes first broadcast more than thirty years ago, we still strongly recommend this book:

John Berger (1972) *Ways of Seeing*, Harmondsworth: Penguin.

Although this book was last revised in 1992 it is still a splendid introduction to visual communication:

John Morgan and Peter Welton (1992) *See What I Mean*, London: Arnold.

Laura Mulvey's most famous paper is 'Visual pleasure and narrative cinema', which was first published in 1975 in *Screen* 16(3) Autumn. You can find the full text at:

http://www.jahsonic.com/LauraMulvey.html

You can read Janice Winship's essay 'Handling sex' in a collection of essays edited by Rosemary Betterton (1987) *Looking On*, London: Pandora.

HISTORICAL MATERIALISM

'A spectre is haunting Europe . . .'
Marx and Engels, *Manifesto of the Communist Party*

In 1848, the German philosopher and journalist Karl Marx and his collaborator and co-writer, the German industrialist Freidrich Engels, published a pamphlet entitled the *Manifesto of the Communist Party*. Although it is a political work, its title is slightly misleading today. By 'party' the authors do not mean an organisation like today's Labour or Conservative Parties, with membership cards, rules, elected officers, and so on, but a movement, a body of opinion, much more like the anti-globalisation or the animal rights movement. The idea of the Communist Party as a formal organisation came later. Again, when we speak of a manifesto now, we usually mean a document drawn up by a candidate or party seeking election and making specific promises for action in the near future, for example cutting taxes or abolishing student university fees. The aims of Marx and Engels' *Communist Manifesto* were much more general and far-reaching.

Marx and Engels claimed to have established the laws by which human society develops – the 'laws of history', analogous to the laws of physics or chemistry. They claimed that history was a science and that by studying it, we could show not only how we come to have the social and political structures that we do, but also how those structures will continue to develop in the future.

They showed that all human societies are based around the production of wealth, whether in the form of agriculture or hunting in the simplest economies or the operations of heavy industry and international commerce, and they described the way in which all societies are divided into economic classes. The class that you belong to depends on the relationship you have to the production of wealth. Thus, in the Middle Ages, when the economy was mainly concerned with agriculture, there were kings, aristocrats, smaller landowners, peasants and serfs. Each of these groups had different economic interests and from time to time they came into conflict as, for example, in England, when Wat Tyler led the Peasants' Revolt in 1381 against the enforcement of the poll tax or when the barons forced King John to sign the Magna Carta in 1215, limiting the powers of the crown in the interests of the aristocracy.

Marx and Engels asserted that the clash of interests between economic classes was the driving force behind social change. As new technologies develop, new ways of creating wealth come into being. These developments create new classes who struggle for power with the established ones. If one class represents the interests of an old-fashioned and inefficient way of working and another those of a new and better system of creating wealth, there arises a conflict between those who have political power but no longer have the economic initiative (the old regime) and the new classes, who have knowledge and wealth but are denied a political voice.

The most obvious example of this, at the time Marx was writing, was the new class of industrialists and businessmen (they were almost without exception men at that time) who were creating unprecedented wealth through the new processes of the industrial revolution. Opposed to their interest was the old ruling class of the landowning aristocracy and gentry. Marx and Engels termed this new class the bourgeoisie, because they typically lived and worked in the towns and cities that were growing at an unprecedented rate as people flooded in to get jobs in the factories and mills. They described how the new class in Britain had begun to wrest power from the old rulers by making parliament more powerful than the monarch, through the English Civil Wars (1642–46 and 1648–59) and the Glorious Revolution of 1688–89 and through parliamentary reforms such as the Great Reform Act of 1832 which took representation away from thinly populated rural seats and redistributed it to more populous urban ones, at the same time extending the right to vote to more and more men. Although this was most advanced in Britain, Marx and Engels were confident that the pattern would be repeated throughout Europe and America as industrialisation spread.

The bourgeois revolution was, however, not the final stage. As well as the bourgeoisie, the new economic system of the industrial world, known as capitalism because it depends on the investment of capital, created new social and economic class, which Marx and Engels termed the proletariat. These are the workers who earn their living in the factories, mines and mills (collectively termed the means of production) owned by the bourgeoisie. Because, unlike the bourgeoisie, they have no wealth to begin with, they can live only by doing work in exchange for wages.

Marx and Engels saw that it was the work of the proletariat that actually created new wealth, although most of that wealth ended up in the pockets of the capitalists – the factory owners, the bourgeoisie. Thus, they felt, the proletariat were being exploited. They were not receiving the full rewards produced by their labour, so they were bound to come into conflict with their employers. Because capitalism was such a successful system, it was bound to continue to grow and, as a result, the great majority of people would soon belong to the proletariat. This huge new class would eventually seize control of the means of production and establish a system of public ownership and control (socialism). This would be so much more efficient than the wasteful competition of capitalism that even higher levels of wealth than before would be created and society would move into its final phase, an economy of plenty for everyone in which work was largely mechanised and where everyone could lead a life of self-fulfilment. This would be the end of the history of class struggle, because all people would now belong to the same class. Marx and Engels called this final stage of society communism: hence the title of their book.

By now you are probably thinking something like, 'This is all very well, but what's it got to do with Communication Studies?'

Although the revolutionary political claims of the *Communist Manifesto* have been hotly contested ever since its publication, and although many people (although not the present authors) think that the collapse of the Soviet Union in the 1980s and 1990s somehow disproved Marx's theory, many of the general ideas in the book are accepted as mainstream theory within the social sciences. One such idea is that society progresses from one stage to another as a result of new knowledge, scientific and technological discoveries and their application to the production of wealth. Another, very powerful, idea is that this process leads inexorably to a better world and that social change over the long run is always for the better. Yet another is the notion that history can be divided into periods, each of which is characterised by a particular style of wealth-creation (what Marx termed a mode of production). Thus in Europe, the classical period (the time of ancient Greece and Rome, when the mode of production was based on slavery) was succeeded by the Middle Ages (when it was agricultural) and this in turn by the modern, capitalist period (industrial). This concept of historical periods, and especially the characterisation of the modern world, underlies many of the critical positions described in this chapter, notably structuralism (see **Structuralism and Poststructuralism**) and postmodernism (see **Postmodernism**). It is important too to stress that this view is strongly challenged as Eurocentric by postcolonial theorists (see **Postcolonialism**), who point out that the European/North American model of history it describes does not fit the history of the rest of the world.

Marxist ideas are also very important in the way we study texts of various kinds. The most important aspect of this is the concept of ideology. Marx and Engels showed that the ideas that are accepted by most people in a given society are those that serve the interests of the rulers, or, as they put it, the dominant ideology of a society is the ideology of the ruling class. This ideology creates a kind of screen, called false consciousness, which prevents people from seeing what is really going on. Marxist critiques of texts seek to expose the underlying power relations and political messages within texts by stripping this away. This technique is also much in evidence in Gender Criticism (see **Gender Criticism**), Discourse Analysis (see **Discourse Analysis**) and Postcolonialism (see **Postcolonialism**) as well as many other critical positions.

Marx's ideas were taken up and developed by many people in many ways. In Russia, Lenin developed a dogmatic but practical version of the theory that aimed specifically at the seizure of state power and was the ideological force behind the Russian revolution of 1917 and the creation of the Soviet Union, the world's first socialist state. After Lenin's death, the official Soviet form of Marxism was codified still more dogmatically by his successor, Josef Stalin, as dialectical and historical materialism and was taught more as a belief system (like a religion) than as a body of critical thought.

Stalin's opponent for the leadership of Russia after Lenin's death was Leon Trotsky. Stalin exiled Trotsky and eventually had him assassinated. However, before his death Trotsky formulated a different, more actively revolutionary version of Marxism and it is from this version that most of the remaining left-wing revolutionary groups in Europe and North America descend.

Both dialectical materialism and Trotskyism have had, and continue to have, some minor influence in academic studies. However, developments of Marxist theory by Western European writers have been more influential. These writers have tended to look for a richer, less simplistic analysis and to avoid the excesses of the Soviet version which many people felt led to the construction of an oppressive dictatorship and to terrible atrocities which eventually discredited it.

In Italy, the leader of the Communist Party, Antonio Gramsci, was imprisoned by the Fascist dictator Benito Mussolini and while in prison wrote a very powerful and influential body of work. Perhaps the most significant single part of this for Communication students is his notion of hegemony. This simply means the way that power is exercised within society. Gramsci's key insight was that in modern societies, the population are controlled not by force or coercion but through their consent, which is obtained by the careful use of mediated communication. And in post-war France, Louis Althusser synthesised Marxism with structuralism (see **Structuralism and Poststructuralism**).

The ideas of Gramsci and Althusser, as well as a number of other theorists, were heavily influential on academic thought at the time that Communication Studies was developing, mainly through the journal *New Left Review*. At this time the journal was edited by Perry Anderson and his book *Considerations on Western Marxism* is a very good place to look for an outline of these ideas.

Consolidation

You can start by reading Karl Marx and Freidrich Engels, *The Communist Manifesto*, especially the section headed 'Bourgeois and Proletarian'. You can find the text at:
http://www.marxists.org/archive/marx/works/1848/communist-manifesto/
There is a good introduction to Louis Althusser's work at:
http://www.colorado.edu/English/ENGL2012Klages/1997althusser.html
Antonio Gramsci's work is not always easy to read, as much of it was written in prison in a deliberately cryptic style. A good place to start finding out about him is:
http://www.marxists.org/archive/gramsci/
Key ideas: bourgeoisie and proletariat, class struggle

PSYCHOANALYSIS

When we say that someone intended to take a particular course of action, we generally mean that they knew they were trying to do it, that they were consciously aware of what they were doing. Consequently, when we look at an instance of communication, we may think we should ask what the speaker or writer intended by it and, if they are available, we might think the easiest way to answer that would be to ask them. However, we would soon discover that people are not always aware of the reasons for their actions, including their communications. People often say things that tell us a great deal about themselves – not because of their conscious intentions, but in spite of them. For example, a husband is pretending, while eating breakfast, that he is happy to go shopping with his wife and does not at all wish to play golf instead. He picks up a piece of toast and asks her to 'Pass the putter'.

Such revealing slips of the tongue (often called 'Freudian slips', after the founder of psychoanalysis, Sigmund Freud) indicate that beyond the conscious awareness of the speaker, there is a mental conflict taking place. Psychoanalysis is largely concerned with revealing the contents of such unconscious thinking. When psychoanalytic critics consider a text, they look not only for its surface meaning (its manifest content) but also for its deeper, hidden meaning (its latent content).

It is important to psychoanalysts that there is no such thing as an accident in human thought and communication. Every human action, however apparently arbitrary, has a meaning and can be explained. The explanation will generally be found in the contents of the unconscious mind.

The unconscious is the part of the mind in which thinking and decision-making go on without our being conscious of them. It comes into being because there are some thoughts, memories and ideas that are too painful for us to acknowledge so we hide them from ourselves. In the popular construction, we 'put them to the back of our minds'. This is the process that Freud called repression. Once a memory or idea has been repressed it is invisible to the person but still affects their thoughts and actions. In this way, it seeks an outlet, or expression, through actions or words. As Freud definitively put it, the repressed returns.

Much of the content of the unconscious is made up of sexual thoughts and memories, particularly from early childhood. Because these are experienced as shaming, they are too painful to be consciously confronted. Despite that, or perhaps because of it, they exercise great influence on us and may make us do things we don't actually understand. The best human example of this phenomenon is the Oedipus complex.

Freud explained the Oedipus complex is this way. The first love object for all children is their mother. As soon as male children come to self-awareness, at around the age of three or four as their language capacity develops, they experience a desire to have their mother's love all to themselves. But they find that they have a rival, their father, who is much more powerful than they are. Thus sons are invariably in conflict with their fathers and fear that if the father finds out their true feelings they will be punished (by castration, according to Freud). The way out of this dilemma is through a process of identifying with the father (being like Dad). If the son successfully achieves this identification, his Oedipus complex is resolved and he is free to develop into an adult man who can seek out an appropriate love object of his own. If he doesn't succeed, the son will be likely to retain characteristics of rebellion, fear of authority, antagonism to male relatives or elder males generally, and dependence on female authority figures.

There is a female version of the Oedipus complex which involves an extra stage: the daughter still starts out with her mother as the primary love object; thus, in addition to the stages her brother has to pass through, she also has to switch her affection from one parent to the other before she can resolve her Oedipus complex by identifying with her mother.

Psychoanalysis, like historical materialism (see **Historical Materialism**), has been changed and developed in many ways by many different theorists and practitioners. It has developed more as a body of critical theory than as a medical technique. As a therapy it is still hotly disputed and is not recognised by mainstream medicine as an appropriate therapeutic approach in many parts of the world. You can't get psychoanalysis on the National Health in the United Kingdom and you can't claim the cost of it from your medical insurance in the United States or in most European countries.

However, it has proved to be an enormously valuable approach in literary and cultural criticism, most notably in Film Studies. Communication theorists and critics may use psychoanalytic methods to interpret texts by identifying telltale signs that indicate a hidden subtext or by identifying

Freudian themes within the text. For example, in the case of Eminem, a critic might suggest that his use of different names (Eminem, Marshall Mathers, Slim Shady) indicates that beneath his aggressively individualist tough guy pose lies a deep uncertainty as to his real identity. They might also suggest that his aggressive lyrics directed towards his mother indicate an unresolved oedipal conflict in which the aggression he was unable to express to his father has been turned against his mother instead.

From its early beginnings psychoanalysis grew rapidly as both a therapy and a body of critical theory. During Freud's lifetime a number of competing branches developed. Some were led by his own pupils, such as Alfred Adler and Carl Gustav Jung, others were led by practitioners influenced by Freud's writings such as Melanie Klein. She, along with other women analysts including Karen Horney, challenged Freud's patriarchal approach and created a feminist perspective within psychoanalysis.

In the 1950s, the French psychoanalyst Jacques Lacan claimed that many of the developments in the field had lost touch with Freud's original perspective. He demanded that analysts should go 'back to Freud' and, influenced heavily by structuralism and semiotics, proposed a new approach which stressed the importance of the influence of others on the development of the individual, particularly through the use of language. For Lacan, in many ways, it is the use of words which lies at the root of human psychology.

Like Freud, Lacan has often been criticised for having an excessively male-centred approach. One of his followers, the Bulgarian analyst Julia Kristeva, who is regarded by many feminists as one of themselves although she has never explicitly described herself as such, placed greater importance on the body. In approaching the relationship between culture and nature in the formation of human experience, Kristeva emphasises the significance of maternal influence in opposition to Lacan's privileging of the 'Law of the Father'.

The psychoanalytic process of unmaking hidden meanings in texts is strongly analogous to the Marxist approach of challenging ideology and false consciousness (see **Historical Materialism**) and strongly informs other critical positions, most notably Gender Criticism (see **Gender Criticism**).

Consolidation

Some of Sigmund Freud's writings are easily accessible to the general reader. We suggest you take a look at Sigmud Freud (1975) *The Psychopathology of Everyday Life*, Harmonds worth: Penguin.

Alternatively you might like to visit the website of the Freud Museum at:

http://www.freud.org.uk/

Jacques Lacan is not an easy read. You can find a good introduction to him and his work at:

http://www.haberarts.com/lacan.htm

or you might prefer to have a look at his ideas as explained in the format of an educational comic book: Darian Leader and Judy Groves (1995) *Lacan for Beginners*, Trumpington: Icon.

A good place to start finding out about Julia Kristeva is:

http://www.cddc.vt.edu/feminism/Kristeva.html

Key ideas: the unconscious, repression, Freudian slips (parapraxes), neurosis

GENDER CRITICISM (INCLUDING FEMINISM, POSTFEMINISM AND QUEER THEORY)

In the 1960s and 1970s, the Anglo-American academic world was swept by a number of movements which shared an interest in the concept of liberation. One model for these movements was the Black civil rights movement in the US, which began as a non-violent campaign of civil disobedience to end the abusive system of segregation under which Black people were denied access to the same public places, jobs and education as whites, and which became a more assertive and confident movement with the advocation of Black Power and Black Consciousness. The other model was the liberation struggles of former colonies, such as the countries of central and southern Africa, for liberation from their imperial master nations (Belgium, Britain, France, Germany, Portugal). In both cases a political programme for real change in the law and government was allied to a change of consciousness, to an emphasis on taking pride in one's liberation. For a moving account of such a change in consciousness, read *The Autobiography of Malcolm X/with the assistance of Alex Hayley* or watch the Spike Lee film *Malcolm X*.

Many women engaged in these struggles, whether as members of an oppressed group or in solidarity with them, became aware that their own status in contrast to that of their male colleagues was unfair and discriminatory. They began to challenge the structures of male oppression and dominance they identified around them and to insist that women have equal rights with men and demand equal respect. At around the time this movement became known as Women's Liberation. Some feminists are still comfortable with that phrase; others are more suspicious of it.

A number of key works of feminism were written around this time but they need to be seen in the context of a history of women's struggle for equal rights. In 1792 Mary Wollstonecraft published the *Vindication of the Rights of Woman*. Although the body of English writing included works by women from much earlier, ranging from the devotional writings of Julian of Norwich to the Restoration playwright and novelist Aphra Behn, Wollstonecraft directly addressed the issues of women's place in society and the injustices of male domination of the economy, politics and the law. She initiated a debate that continued throughout the nineteenth century and which led, among other things, to the foundation, in 1905, of the Women's Social and Political Union which campaigned for women to be able to vote in elections.

By the dawn of the twentieth century although there were – and still are – many struggles to be won by women against patriarchy, the struggle had begun in earnest. In the sphere of cultural production a new sensibility, prefiguring the 1960s notion that 'the personal is the political' can be seen in the writings of Virginia Woolf (*A Room of One's Own*). By 1949 this had become a conscious attempt to address the situation of women at a fundamental, philosophical level with the publication by Simone de Beauvoir of *Le Deuxième Sexe*. De Beauvoir famously asserted that 'one is not born, but rather becomes, a woman' (de Beauvoir 1988: 259). In other words, the inferiority of women's situation and status comes about not because of their inherently weak and frail 'feminine' characteristics but because it is socially and politically created by the structures in which they grow up. These perceptions were to be enormously influential on the later feminist writers and on the whole development of critical theory in the second half of the twentieth century.

The women's liberation generation made feminist criticism mainstream. The writings of Betty Friedan, Germaine Greer and Andrea Dworkin, diverse as they are, have established that any critique that ignores the situation of women and gender politics is incomplete and outdated. A generation of academic critics has grown up taking for granted notions of women's independence and importance that were hotly contested when they were asserted in the 1960s.

In practical terms, this has produced a large body of criticism of the ways in which women are portrayed and stereotyped in cultural representation, notably in advertising (see **Visual Rhetorics**). A steady barrage of such criticism has now created a climate in which the routine portrayal of women as housewives and carers, while men are characterised as active achievers, is not acceptable in much mainstream advertising. Women are much more likely than before to be represented as independent achievers and social superiors, for example the woman director in the Kenko coffee television advertisements. Many of these advertisements are built on television audience's expectation that men will occupy managerial positions in the workplace, which is then overturned by the revelation of the woman occupying the superior managerial role.

Humour is created out of the reversal and challenge of old stereotypes.

Recent years have seen a rise of 'postfeminism' in which women have sought to repossess some of the old stereotyped images and use them playfully, knowingly and ironically in order to reclaim them for women. A writer sometimes associated with this approach is Camille Paglia, who championed the work of Madonna as 'true feminism' – strong and assertive as opposed to what she characterised as the whining, complaining tone of much women's writing, notably that of Andrea Dworkin.

Another form of gender-based criticism that has transformed our understanding of texts, communication and culture is gay writing. The late twentieth century witnessed a dramatic transformation of the cultural situation of lesbians and gay men. Although, like the women's movement, it has still a lot of battles left to fight, in Europe and North America, particularly in academia, we have seen a change from a time when male homosexual activity was punishable by imprisonment to one in which civil partnerships between lesbians and gay men are a legal reality in some states of the United States, and from a time when homosexuality was considered shameful and disgusting to the Gay Pride marches that defy prejudice in many western cities.

Gay and lesbian criticism has uncovered a rich seam of gay references in texts, such as the homoerotic element present in many supposedly 'tough guy' films. It is not unusual to see such 'revelations' appear in mainstream media: in the 1994 film *Sleep With Me* Quentin Tarantino makes a cameo appearance in which he delivers a speech where he forcefully uncovers the homoerotic subtext of *Top Gun* (1986): 'You think it's a story about a bunch of fighter pilots. . . . It is a story about a man's struggle with his own homosexuality. It is! That is what *Top Gun* is about, man.' Gay and lesbian criticism has also created a climate in which texts openly celebrating alternative sexualities, such as *Gimme Gimme Gimme* or *Will and Grace*, are acceptable in mainstream media. Economics has played a key role as well: in October

2004 the US industry newspaper *Television Week* was able to report that 'Analyst firm Witeck-Combs wrote that the estimated 15 million gays and lesbians in the United States enjoyed a 2003 buying power of $485 billion'.

One of the key sites for struggle for any marginalised or persecuted group is language: both the language you use about yourself and the language other people use to refer to you, to praise you or to demonise you. Whereas in the late 1960s and early 1970s the gay community had used the term 'gay' as a non-gender specific term to describe (and potentially unite) all homosexual people, a decade later radical feminist groups reclaimed the word 'lesbian'. Regularly used as a pejorative term during the 1950s and 1960s, the word was rehabilitated as both an accurate descriptive term and as a source of pride for an emerging collective consciousness.

In a similar way the previously pejorative term 'queer' has been reclaimed by both activist and academic communities. The success of the television programme *Queer Eye for the Straight Guy* (in both the US and UK) is but one index of how the word 'queer' has been rehabilitated by the gay community. It's also an index of how comfortable mainstream media is with broadcasting programmes featuring openly gay – queer – men. But the presence of gay men and lesbians as characters in television programmes is not without its inequalities. It is now the case that gay male characters appear routinely in television dramas, particularly soap operas, where their being gay is not an issue or a storyline. In other words, they have moved from being either invisible or despised, to being an 'issue' or a problem, to being a token gay character (written into the script in a bogus interpretation of inclusiveness), to being a police officer or a farmer or a chef who just happens to be a gay man. But lesbians have not necessarily enjoyed a similar integration into British television drama: in soap operas such as *Brookside* and *EastEnders* lesbian characters have been written into the scripts more in the spirit of titillation (quite possibly a manifestation of heterosexual men's lesbian fantasies).

Recent times have witnessed the emergence of Queer Theory. Probably most visible in the context of a New Queer

Cinema in, for example, Todd Haynes' films such as *Poison* (1991), *Velvet Goldmine* (1998) and *Far From Heaven* (2002), Queer Theory represents not only a way forward to gain productive insights into all kinds of texts but also continuity with earlier queer writers. In 1990 Eve Kosofsky Sedgwick argued that a queering of texts would constitute a move away from a 'minoritising' examination of homosexuals and homosexuality to a 'universalising' investigation of how sexuality in general is constructed and how that is a key component in power relations within any community of whatever gender preference. In that sense, Queer Theory could represent a realisation of Michel Foucault's call for a 'general economy of pleasure not based on heterosexual norms' (Foucault 1980: 191) (see **Discourse Analysis** and **Structuralism and Poststructuralism**).

Used as an analytical tool, Queer Theory offers a way of looking afresh at texts previously thought to be resolutely heterosexual. Just as the perspectives offered by writers such as Edward Said (see **Postcolonialism**) offer us new ways of examining the texts of the colonial era and of seeing them in a different, more informed light, so too Queer Theory offers new insights into all kinds of texts once they have been queered.

Consolidation

Mary Wollstonecraft's *A Vindication of the Rights of Woman* can be read online at:
   http://www.swan.ac.uk/poli/texts/wollstonecraft/vindicon.htm
   Take a look at Simone de Beauvoir (1998) *The Second Sex*, London: Pan
   or look her up at:
   http://www.philosophypages.com/ph/beav.htm
   Andrea Dworkin has an online library of her work. You can find it at:
   http://www.nostatusquo.com/ACLU/dworkin/OnlineLibrary.html

A book that was very influential on the growth of the women's movement in the 1990s is Naomi Wolf (1990) *The Beauty Myth: How Images of Beauty are Used against Women*, London: Vintage.

Germaine Greer wrote perhaps the most influential book of the 1960s: *The Female Eunuch*. Some of it might now seem dated but it is still a powerful book. Germaine Greer (2003) *The Female Eunuch*, London: Flamingo.

Camille Paglia is best known for her 1990 book *Sexual Personae: Art and Decadence from Nefertiti to Emily Dickinson*, London: Yale University Press.

But you can get a feel for her writing by dipping into this collection of her writings – Camille Paglia (1995) *Vamps and Tramps*, London: Penguin.

You can read a useful introduction to New Queer Cinema online at:

http://www.glbtq.com/arts/new_queer_cinema.html

Key ideas: feminism, postfeminism, gay and lesbian criticism, Queer Theory

STRUCTURALISM AND POSTSTRUCTURALISM

Structuralism is the name given to theories that seek to explain their subject in terms of the interrelatedness of all its parts. De Saussure's structural linguistics states that no sign can have a meaning on its own, but can function only as part of a system of signs (see **Semiotics**). A word, for example, makes sense only as part of a language. No word could exist without a language to which it belonged; it would simply be a sound in the air or a scratch on paper, without meaning.

Linguistics is perhaps the most obvious example of structure creating the possibility for the existence of individual objects, actions or events, but the principle extends to all fields of knowledge. The French anthropologist Claude Lévi-Strauss was heavily influenced by de Saussure and produced a structural anthropology in which he sought to explain kinship systems, rituals and all other forms of the behaviour of people within particular societies as components of a larger structure which comprised the society as a whole.

For over thirty years Lévi-Strauss undertook fieldwork visiting and studying North and South America Indian peoples. He collected and analysed folk tales or myths from these peoples. Extrapolating from his field studies he claimed that a structural study of myth would reveal common elements in myths from many different cultures. He asserted that myth was made out of units just like a language. And while some people assembled these units in one way, another set of people would assemble it differently. For example, in one culture there's a story about a fish inside a man; in another culture there's a story about a man inside a fish. Both stories contain the same elements, something simply gets rearranged as story elements are used by and in different cultures.

What Lévi-Strauss was doing from the 1930s to the 1970s was in many ways a continuation of what Vladimir Propp had done in Russia a little earlier. Analysing Russian folk tales Propp was able to identify the thirty-one plot elements they all had in common, and the sequence in which they occurred. (In this way we could regard Hollywood producers and agents as unconscious structuralists with their three-act film structures, classic narrative arcs and cipher-like concept of character.)

However, it would be a mistake to think of structuralism as beginning with de Saussure and linguistics or Propp and folk tales. In fact, many of the major theorists of the nineteenth and early twentieth centuries can be considered structuralists, including Marx (see **Historical Materialism**) and Freud (see **Psychoanalysis**). Historical materialism explains the actions of individuals or groups in terms of their relationship to society as a whole, and specifically to the clash of interests between social classes which Marx saw as underlying all of history. Psychoanalysis explains individual actions in terms of their relationship to the unconscious. In both cases the structure is the source of explanation for the individual act or event.

Structuralism was dominant in the social sciences, particularly Sociology, throughout much of the second half of the twentieth century and is still the position of many theorists.

Recently, evolutionary psychologists have offered an explanation of animal and human behaviour grounded in the imperatives of genetics and natural selection. This is a structuralist position.

In the middle of the twentieth century, however, structuralism was challenged by a number of people, the best known being the French philosophers Michel Foucault, Jacques Derrida and Jean-François Lyotard. Each of these, in different ways, challenged the notion that a *complete* explanation of anything is possible. Previous thinkers, they contended, including the structuralists, had believed that their theories and methods could disclose the whole truth, but, on the contrary, no such truth was possible. In this they drew on the writings of the nineteenth-century German philosopher Friedrich Nietzsche who had asked 'Whose truth are we dealing with?' His understanding that truth is always linked to (political) power became, in Foucault's writing, the notion of *savoir/pouvoir* – knowledge/power.

These writers and their followers became known as poststructuralists. Poststructuralism is not simply a rejection of structuralism, returning to explanations based on individual units, rather than their systemic relationships, but goes further. Whereas structuralists asserted that truth could not be found in the study of individual components but only in their relationships, so the poststructuralists insisted that even in those relationships no ultimate truth was to be found.

Truth is always provisional and temporary, awaiting a new interpretation. For structuralists, the basis of meaning was to be found in difference – a sign, for example, means what it does precisely because it does not mean what any of the other signs in the system mean. This led Derrida to coin the term *différance*, which, in French, combines the sense of 'difference' and 'deferral'.

Poststructuralism is closely linked to postmodernism (see **Postmodernism**), since both terms refer to a view that challenges the very notion of fixed truth or reality, as well as the concept of the self as an entity, independent of communication and perception.

Consolidation

You can check out Claude Lévi-Strauss at:
http://www.mnsu.edu/emuseum/information/biography/
klmno/levi-strauss_claude.html
Vladimir Propp's structural analysis of fairy stories can be approached by taking his model from:
http://mural.uv.es/vifresal/Propp.htm
and applying it to a story or film with which you are familiar.

You can get a lot of the gist of Michel Foucault's approach by reading the opening chapters of his books. We particularly suggest you look at.

Michel Foucault (1971) *Madness and Civilisation: a History of Insanity in the Age of Reason*, London: Routledge
or:

Michel Foucault (1991) *Discipline and Punish: the Birth of the Prison*, London: Penguin.

POSTMODERNISM

There is often confusion among students about the differences between modernism, modernity, postmodernism and post-modernity. We offer here a concise description of the main ways in which these terms are used.

Modernity refers to the historical period that begins in Europe in the fifteenth and sixteenth centuries and continues to the present day. By contrast to the medieval period that went before, this is characterised by people moving from the countryside to the towns; industrial production becoming a more important part of the economy than agricultural pro-duction; the use of machinery and engines; the rise of a new social class whose power comes not from inheritance, but from innovation and industry; the replacement of feudalism by democracy; and the rise of nationalism and the nation-state. It is the age of science, of a decline in religion and an increasing belief in humanism and progress.

Modernism refers much more specifically to a movement in art, design and ideas which began around the start of the twentieth century. It encompasses a range of styles in painting, sculpture, literature and architecture, as well as a more general approach to life and philosophy. It is centrally concerned with the notion of progress. Modernist works are self-consciously new and innovative. Examples include the poetry of T. S. Eliot, the novels of James Joyce and the arts of Pablo Picasso.

Perhaps the art most exemplary of modernism is the 'International Style' of modern architecture. This proposed that buildings should be of their time and function, and not tied to tradition or local style. New materials, such as steel and concrete, should be used and designs should be simple and functional. Roofs should be flat and decoration should be avoided. Because modernism in architecture is associated with political ideas of equality and socialism, standardisation was also an important theme. The outcome of all this was the tower block estate, in which rows of similar high-rise blocks contained a number of similar apartments. The design was seen to be rational and democratic, as well as being symbolic of progress and egalitarianism.

Of course, tower blocks did not please many of the people who lived in them. This was at least partly because of factors other than their design principles, such as poor building standards, exploitative contractors and social factors that coerced people into them against their wishes, but it was also an indication that people wanted less uniformity and more individuality than the buildings permitted. By the 1970s, architects were beginning to question the international style and gradually new types of building became common, in which decoration, quotations from local and vernacular styles, low-rise and individualistic motifs appear. Think of any recent supermarket development: it is likely to be single- or at most twin-storeyed, and to feature pitched roofs and decorative touches of mock classical, Georgian or even medieval architecture.

Such architecture, and similar turnings away from modernism in other arts, became characterised as postmodernist, not in the sense that they relate to a later period in history, but rather that they take their meaning from their opposition to modernism. Modernism is characteristically purposeful, rational, politically engaged (often, though not exclusively, on the left) and above all serious. Modernists in art and architecture generally believe strongly that their work has a moral dimension and is too important to be treated lightly. Conversely, postmodernists choose to take a deliberately playful approach to their art, to employ humour, fancifulness and irony.

Charles Jencks identifies the origins of postmodernity in the shift in advanced economies away from the manufacture of goods to the processing of information. Where industrial society imposed large rigid structures on life and society, the information-based culture, he contends, emphasises individuality and flexibility.

From the idea of postmodernism, we may now look at the idea of postmodernity. If modernism and postmodernism are artistic and intellectual movements or positions, can we say that modernity and postmodernity refer to the times in which they take place? Emphatically not. Partly because the beginnings of modernity can be dated back to at least the fifteenth century, while modernism is largely a twentieth-century phenomenon but, more importantly, because modernism and postmodernism exist side by side and in dialogue with each other. If postmodernist works are characterised by playfulness, quotation, self-reference, irreverence and irony, we can point to works from the early modern period that seem to prefigure them, such as Cervantes' novel *Don Quixote* (in which the leading character reads the book in which he appears) or Jan van Eyck's painting of the Arnolfi betrothal, in the background of which is a mirror reflecting the artist himself, looking into the scene and also looking back at the viewer.

None the less, writers such as Charles Jencks and Jean-François Lyotard have proposed that we now live in a condition of postmodernity. For many commentators, this is principally a matter of the loss of authority of science. Whereas until the early twentieth century scientific and

technological progress seemed to be unquestionably good
things, the last hundred years have taught us the downside of
relying on continuous development and innovation. Science
has produced great advances in medicine, for example, but
also weapons of such destructiveness that we are now fright-
ened of our own technology.

Nor have supposed advances always turned out to be the
unquestionable good they seemed at first. Insecticides and
intensive farming methods that were once thought to lead to
an abundance of food for all have resulted in environmental
devastation. Technology seems out of control and often seems
to cause more trouble than it solves. The invention of the
World Wide Web at first seemed a dream come true of uni-
versal communication and access to information. While much
of that is being realised, it is doing so alongside greatly
expanded opportunities for paedophiles, pornographers and
terrorists. Science is thus becoming no longer the privileged
discourse of our culture but merely one competing among
many – we are seeing a revival of religious belief and also of
supernatural ideas (exemplified by the New Age movement).

Alongside the loss of science's central explanatory role
within our culture, we can observe a failure of any single,
overarching explanation of our life. Marxism as a realisable
political doctrine seems to have failed, Freudian psychoanalysis is challenged from many directions, and neither
socialism nor free market capitalism seems to have the
answers to our economic problems.

Lyotard calls such overarching explanations 'grand narratives' and proposes that the condition of postmodernity is one
in which we can no longer give credence to any of them. We
might make use of concepts drawn from psychoanalysis, for
example, but we cannot subscribe to the whole body of psychoanalytic theory. The notion of the Oedipus complex may
offer a useful explanation of one text but that does not mean
that it will be valuable or appropriate for the next text we
examine. Of course, it could just be the case that the construction of psychoanalysis as one single body of thought is
yet another example of a grand narrative mentality. For

example, psychoanalysis itself contained many diverse strands of often divergent thought right from the outset. While there was a world of difference between psychoanalysis as conceived of and practised by Alfred Adler, Sigmund Freud, Carl Jung and Wilhelm Reich it is still referred to as if it were the one undivided school of thought. Maybe the adopting of a postmodernist perspective is simply to perceive things as they have always been.

Consolidation

Charles Jencks wrote an interesting and nicely illustrated book about postmodernism: Charles Jencks (1989) *What is Postmodernism?*, London: Academy. You can look him up at:

http://www.eng.fju.edu.tw/Literary_Criticism/postmodernism/jencks.htm

In 1979 Jean-François Lyotard wrote *The Postmodern Condition: A Report on Knowledge*, which you can find in Jean-François Lyotard (1984) *The Postmodern Condition*, Manchester: Manchester University Press. The first five chapters are reproduced here:

http://www.marxists.org/reference/subject/philosophy/works/fr/lyotard.htm

Key ideas: modernity, postmodernity, modernism, postmodernism, irony

POSTCOLONIALISM

Critical theory has revolutionised the ways in which we think about cultures and texts in a number of ways. Perhaps the most important is the bringing to bear on them of new perspectives. One outstanding example of this is the growth of postcolonial sensibility. This takes one of two forms: (1) the objects under consideration (the films, advertisements, novels, clothes designs, or any other text we want to interrogate) may remain the same but will be subjected to a different form of interrogation; or (2) the very objects deemed appropriate for analysis may themselves be challenged.

The outstanding example of the first approach is the work of the late Palestinian literary critic, Edward Said. In his views on what is good or interesting literature Said is conservative, rather more than most critics of the late twentieth century. He is a defender of the traditional canon of great works of world literature, particularly the western literary tradition, and specifically decries the practice of giving equal consideration to popular and high culture.

At the same time, he offers a critique of such works from an entirely radical perspective. While the nineteenth-century English novel was written about and for certain groups and classes of people, Said points out that their lives took place in a wider context which included many things and people excluded from the world of the novel.

Said's analysis of Jane Austen's novel *Mansfield Park* is a good example of his approach. The novel is set entirely in England and revolves around the lives of 'respectable' middle-class people and the country estate named in the title. However Said points out that the money that pays for this luxurious home comes from sugar plantations in the West Indies. At the time the novel is set that could only mean that Sir Thomas Bertram is a slave owner and that all the refined sentiment and polite society depicted by Austen is paid for by human misery and subjugation. To read the novel from this perspective is to see the characters and their actions in a completely new light. A postcolonial reading of the novel reveals the slave trade as its absent presence, the subject we notice because it is absent, because the characters are silent about it. As Said observes: 'In time there would no longer be a dead silence when slavery was spoken of, and the subject became central in a new under-standing of what Europe was' (Said 1978: 96). This does not make it a novel 'about' slavery in the sense that, say, *Uncle Tom's Cabin* nor even *Huckleberry Finn* is about slavery, but it offers a radically changed perspective on the story.

The alternative, almost opposite, response to Said's to imperialism in criticism is to challenge the canon itself and insist on the analysis of texts produced by the culturally or colonially subjugated. This has perhaps worked best in the study of film. Although this area of academia is still predominantly concerned with the work of the European and English-speaking world, there is growing interest in the cinemas of Africa, South America, the Middle East and Asia.

Consolidation

Edward Said's most famous book is *Orientalism*; the most recent edition published is Edward Said (1994) *Orientalism*, New York: Vintage.

You can find out more about both him and *Orientalism* at: http://www.english.emory.edu/Bahri/Orientalism.html

6 FURTHER READING

This chapter offers you some further reading. Many other books that are intended as preliminary reading direct their readers to long lists of further readings. There's a certain macho motivation to these long reading lists or bibliographies: the longer the list, the more reading the authors have done. The sheer length of many books' bibliographies can prove daunting to new Communication Studies students. We remain guided by the amount of time you can be expected to devote to reading about and around Communication Studies in the time you have between school or college and university. In the previous chapter, The Communication Studies Toolkit, we gave you some very precise additional readings you could undertake to consolidate your learning. These were rarely whole books; most often they were small sections or chapters of books or parts of websites. This was in line with the idea of providing you with a book that could be read in bite-sized chunks. If we had recommended a large number of books it's highly unlikely that you'd actually manage to read them all in the time available to you. Worse still, you would run the risk of not having a reasonably clear picture of what it was you were about to embark upon studying in the next three years.

In that spirit we offer you our Further Reading. We want these readings to be resources you can use now – before you begin your formal studies – and resources to which you can refer once settled into your undergraduate studies. We are recommending only three further texts or resources. One is an introductory textbook (*Beginning Theory*); one is an anthology of key readings (*Communication Studies: The Essential Resource*); and one is a website (The Media and Communications Studies Site hosted by the University of Wales at Aberystwyth).

We are going to give you a guided tour of those parts of these resources which we feel will reinforce and consolidate the learning you've already achieved. This will take the form of precise page, section or chapter references; those pages, sections or chapters not referred to are not relevant to your introduction to Communication Studies. In this chapter we'll also give you cross-references to sections in this book (in **bold**).

PETER BARRY (2002) *BEGINNING THEORY*, MANCHESTER: MANCHESTER UNIVERSITY PRESS

This book was written as an introduction to literary and cultural theory. It was first published in 1995 and a second, revised edition was published in 2002. We grant that the book is an introduction to the analysis of literary texts – and all of its worked examples use literary texts – but what it says and how it says it are eminently transferable to Communication Studies. Furthermore, it offers succinct and insightful consolidations of what we outlined for you in The Communication Studies Toolkit.

Here are our page-by-page recommendations of what to read in this excellent book.

Pages 6–8 represent an excellent introduction to how the uninitiated should approach theory, containing as it does a useful set of health warnings. As Barry clearly advises, 'What *is* difficult is the language of theory. Many of the major writers on theory are French, so that much of what we read is in translation, sometimes of a rather clumsy nature' (Barry 2002: 7).

Pages 21–31 give you a history of theory before theory; Barry is at pains to point out that theory didn't emerge in the twentieth century. He surveys key theoretical moments from Aristotle to F. R. Leavis. Although his survey is located in literary history it still provides a very useful background to any contemporary intellectual study. Given that many histories of Communication Studies are quite partial (see **Which Theory for Communication Studies?**) reading these pages is a useful exercise in seeing how much of what we feel we know is simply what someone has told us. In that sense, all knowledge is simply a story, albeit a story with which we agree.

Pages 39–59 give you a useful consolidation of your previous learning about structuralist writers such as Ferdinand de Saussure, Claude Lévi-Strauss and Roland Barthes. Barry also gives you some useful exercises to do to reinforce your learning further. If you are coming to Communication Studies at undergraduate level from 'A' level studies in English Literature these will prove most useful in effecting that transition (see **Structuralism and Poststructuralism**).

Pages 61–65 are about structuralism and poststructuralism and offer a keen distinction between the two (see **Structuralism and Poststructuralism**).

Pages 65–70 are about the work of Roland Barthes and Jacques Derrida (see **Semiotics** and **Structuralism and Poststructuralism**).

Pages 81–85 offer you an introduction to modernism and postmodernism (see **Postmodernism**).

Pages 85–94 consolidate Barry's introduction to postmodernism with a survey of the work of the German critical theorist Jürgen Habermas and the French philosophers Jean-François Lyotard and Jean Baudrillard. Lyotard and Baudrillard are essential reading for Communication Studies students, Habermas is less important, unless you are taking an undergraduate Communication Studies programme that has Cultural Studies or Cultural Policy elements or modules (see **Postmodernism**).

Pages 96–98 are a brief introduction to psychoanalysis. They are followed by introductions to a number of psychoanalytic writers (see **Psychoanalysis**).

Pages 98–102 reinforce Barry's explanation of Freud's method and offer a summary of a case study from one of Freud's key works, *The Psychopathology of Everyday Life*. The case study, 'The Forgetting of Foreign Words', appears in full on pages 65–69 of *Communication Studies: The Essential Resource*.

Pages 102–5 offer you some of the main criticisms made of Freud and Freudian analysis.

Pages 108–15 are an introduction to the work of Jacques Lacan. As we've said (see **Psychoanalysis**) Lacan is not an easy read; and while we would always argue that there is ultimately no substitute for reading an author's original words, in Lacan's case simple introductions can prove most useful.

Pages 115–18 are a worked example of Lacanian methods. Barry uses Lacan to analyse Edgar Allan Poe's story 'The Purloined Letter'. Although Barry uses the analysis of a literary text to exemplify his explanation of Lacan, this is extremely useful. Indeed, many theorists' work can appear dull or useless when presented in dry theoretical terms; it's often the case that the work comes alive (or becomes something you understand and can work with) only in such an application. Theory isn't meant to make life, the world and experiences difficult; it's meant to illuminate them, to make them more, not less, understandable.

Pages 121–3 provide the historical background to feminism (see **Gender Criticism**).

Pages 130–4 cover feminist criticisms of psychoanalysis.

Pages 134–6 offer another excellent worked example. The literary text used here is *Wuthering Heights* and it is given a feminist analysis.

Pages 140–2 offer an account of lesbian feminism.

Pages 143–8 introduce Queer Theory (see **Gender Criticism**).

Pages 150–3 are taken up with another excellent worked example: here the love poetry of the First World War is analysed from a gay/lesbian perspective (see **Gender Criticism**).

Pages 156–8 provide a sound introduction to Marxism, from its origins and first principles (see **Historical Materialism**).

Pages 163–6 offer an insight into the work of Louis Althusser. Just as Lacan famously argued that psychoanalysts should go back to Freud so too was Althusser famous for insisting that historical materialism and self-styled Marxists should return to Marx. Here Barry covers not only the work of Althusser himself but also those contemporary Marxists who have been influential in the later decades of the twentieth century (see **Historical Materialism**).

Pages 168–70 contain yet another excellent worked example, this time a Marxist analysis of William Shakespeare's *Twelfth Night*.

Page 192 introduces postcolonialism and postcolonialist criticism (see **Postcolonialism**).

Pages 192–4 provide useful historical background to postcolonialism.

Pages 200–1 are taken up with another of Barry's worked examples. This time he takes you through Edward Said's postcolonialist critique of Jane Austen's *Mansfield Park*, which we referred to in our introduction to postcolonialism (see **Postcolonialism**).

ANDREW BECK, PETER BENNETT AND PETER WALL (2004) *COMMUNICATION STUDIES: THE ESSENTIAL RESOURCE*, LONDON: ROUTLEDGE

This book is built on the bite-sized chunks of reading principle: it is an anthology, a collection of extracts from key works of or about Communication Studies. The longest extract takes up seven pages, the shortest barely fills half a page, and most extracts are only a couple of pages long. The book includes extracts from some key writers on Communication Studies whose work is sometimes difficult to find these days. It also includes extracts from many writers whose work is often referred to by commentators but is rarely quoted from. Just as Lacan and Althusser urged us to go back to Freud and Marx respectively, this book frequently does just that. In addition, many of the extracts are taken from somewhat un-likely sources (such as novels or film and television scripts or popular journalism); but nevertheless they offer eminently useful worked examples of how texts can be examined, analysed and evaluated from a Communication Studies perspective.

The book consists of 100 numbered readings so in this guided tour we will refer you to extract numbers rather than to page numbers.

To consolidate your reading about and understanding of what Communication Studies actually is, read extracts 7 (John Fiske's explanation of the process and semiotics approaches to the study of communication); 11 (Denis McQuail and Sven Windahl's explanation of the Mathematical Theory of Communication); 85 (an early attempt to define the study of communication from Colin Cherry's *On Human Communication*); 86 (Raymond Williams' exploration of the multifaceted character of communication); 87 (Judith Williamson's extension of Communication Studies into the world of consumption); 88 (Denis McQuail and Sven Windahl's admonitions about communication models and communication modelling); 89 (John Lye's account of how Roman Jakobson succeeded in synthesising the supposedly contrary process and semiotic schools of Communication Studies); 97 (Basil Bernstein's explanation of how one of the key means of human communication – speech – functions in terms of class membership); 98 (Michael Moore's biting satire on people's assumptions which are based on race and ethnicity); and 99 (Anthony P. Cohen's explanation of how a 'commitment to a common body of symbols' becomes the social glue which holds community together) (see **Which Theory for Communication Studies?**).

To understand better key notions in and aspects of intrapersonal communication, interpersonal communication and group communication, read extracts 12 (John Morgan and Peter Welton's explanation of Osgood and Schramm's model of interpersonal communication); 17 (an extract from Brett Easton Ellis's novel *American Psycho* which is a searing and graphic exploration of self-image and self-presentation in advanced capitalist consumer society); 18 (Mary Ragan's survey of the connection between self-esteem and gender); 23 (an extract from Erving Goffman's *The Presentation of Self in Everyday Life*); 24 (a succinct introduction to social interaction from Richard Dimbleby and Graeme Burton); 28 (an extract from Peter Hartley's key work *Interpersonal Communication*); 29 (some sage words about communication from Eric Berne, founder of Transactional Analysis); and

36 (an insight into how power functions in groups from Peter Hartley's *Group Communication*) (see **From Intrapersonal Communication to Interpersonal Communication to Group Communication** and **Gender Criticism**).

For a useful reinforcement of your understanding of aspects of non-verbal communication, read extracts 25 (Andrew Ellis and Geoffrey Beattie on non-verbal codes of communication); 26 (an explanation of the roles of non-verbal communication from Michael Argyle's classic text *The Psychology of Interpersonal Behaviour*); and 27 (an illustrated guide to the geography of non-verbal communication's meanings from Desmond Morris) (see **Non-Verbal Communication**).

To extend your understanding of how gender influences interpersonal communication, read extract 30 (from Deborah Tannen's writings about conversational style between men and women (see **Verbal Communication** and **Gender Criticism**).

To gain further insights into how communication functions within organisations, read extract 37 (Gerald Cole's concise summary of key concepts used in observing and theorising about leadership and groups within working organisations) (see **Organisational Communication**).

We argued in chapter 4 of this book that the very notion of what mass communication is by no means fixed or stable. Thus it should come as no great surprise to find that readings of mass communication are often controversial. It should also come as no surprise to discover which mass communication objects are chosen for analysis. A key feature of television schedules and popular newspapers is celebrity. For two interesting dissections of celebrity, read extracts 80 (Julie Burchill on Kurt Cobain) and 81 (Ellis Cashmore on David Beckham). For an early piece of work on popular television, read extract 82 (John Fiske on television game shows). A debate within and about mass communication concerns the question of value. Traditional discussions about value in cultural products have been organised around an opposition which pairs high cultural products (elite products) with minority audiences and low cultural products (popular products) with mass audiences. This opposition between high and low culture (sometimes called the two cultures debate) has provided commentators with endless opportunities for discussion about mass communication. This debate is at the heart of any study of mass communication within a Communication Studies programme (and is highly likely to be the subject of coursework within your undergraduate studies). To follow this debate from its origins to its contemporary expression we suggest you read the following extracts: 54 (Dick Hebdige kicks off with an introduction to some of the key figures who have researched culture); 55 (Raymond Williams defines ideology and examines the role it plays in thinking about the relationship between culture and society); 56 (Matthew Arnold offers his classic definition of high culture); 57 (Raymond Williams updates the debate to the mid-1960s); 58 (Melvyn Bragg demonstrates that the debate was still very much alive in the year 2000); 59 (D. J. Taylor saw no reason to think the debate was over and done with by the year 2002); 60 (Robert Eaglestone examines one of the notions about which the debate agonises – the canon: the body of supposedly universally recognised great works of art); and 61 (Paul Taylor introduces you to the ideas of Pierre Bourdieu, who coined the term 'cultural capital' to describe the way people's knowledge of and about art defines their membership of a social class) (see **Mass Communication**).

To consolidate your understanding of semiotics, read extracts 8 (a succinct introduction by Pierre Guiraud); 9 (an extract from Roland Barthes, *Elements of Semiology*); 10 (a terrific elaboration of the ideas of de Saussure, Peirce and Barthes, which concludes with a semiotic analysis of social groups); 14 (an example of Barthes' semiotic analysis in action, here examining how the Romans have been portrayed (or constructed) in film); and 64 (an extract from David Lodge's novel *Nice Work*, featuring a dialogue between an industrialist who knows nothing about semiotics and an academic who routinely uses semiotics to understand the world in which she lives) (see **Semiotics**).

We have referred to the work of Ludwig Wittgenstein a number of times. To get a flavour of how he writes, read extract 3 (Wittgenstein on the relationship between language and the world) (see **Verbal Communication** and **Discourse Analysis**).

We have previously recommended John Berger's classic work *Ways of Seeing*. To get a flavour of how he writes, read extract 2 (which examines how what we believe governs what we see and how we interpret what we see) (see **Visual Rhetorics**).

While we would argue that there is no substitute for reading Marx's own words, this collection features extracts from two very readable works. In the course of a fascinating work that uses classic Marxist theory to investigate architecture and its relation to the underlying ideological structures, Jonathan Hale offers a useful introduction to Marxist thinking (extract 62). In 1970 Ernst Fischer published an invaluable work which sought to cut through the fog of mystification that surrounded much so-called Marxist writing of the time – *Marx in His Own Words*. Read extract 63 for an excellent summary of a concept key not only to Marxist thought but also to analyses of consumer society – commodity fetishism (see **Historical Materialism**).

To reinforce your understanding of Freud, read extracts 19 (from Mick Underwood's Communication and Cultural Studies website, which both summarises Freud's concept of the human personality and offers key criticisms of Freud's ideas); 20 (the full text of Freud's 'The Forgetting of Foreign Words' from his *The Psychopathology Of Everyday Life*); and 21 (in an extract from the script of the film *Analyze This* you see how understanding Freud can enhance our enjoyment of popular film) (see **Psychoanalysis**).

To extend your understanding of feminism, read extracts 40 (Liesbet van Zoonen's elegant exposition of feminist scholarship); 65 (an extract from Germaine Greer's classic feminist call to arms *The Female Eunuch*); 66 (Yvonne Tasker's concise explanation of what is understood by postfeminism); 67 (Camille Paglia's rather more radical, not to say controversial, application of postfeminism which culminates in her claim that Madonna was 'the true feminist'); and 79 (Janice

Winship's feminist analysis of the gendered character of television advertisements) (see **Gender Criticism**).

For further insights into structuralism, read extracts 5 (in an early project to introduce ideas about semiotics and structuralism to the UK Terence Hawkes gets to the heart of what it means to think structurally); and 6 (Umberto Eco reads the James Bond novels of Ian Fleming from a structuralist perspective) (see **Structuralism and Poststructuralism**).

Postmodernism is a distinctly fluid and slippery idea. Accordingly, writings about postmodernism are often fluid and slippery. So it shouldn't be at all surprising that many contemporary commentators' use of the term 'postmodernism' should sometimes be confusing. For a tight explanation of postmodernism as characterised by Jean-François Lyotard, read extract 68 (the entry on Lyotard from John Lechte's great resource *Fifty Key Contemporary Thinkers*). For an eloquent explanation of why postmodernism has made so much of contemporary writing insecure and jittery, read extract 69 (Alan Bryman's description of the ramifications of postmodernism for writing). And for a lovely worked example of a postmodernist reading of contemporary phenomena, read extract 70 (Baudrillard's extrapolation from his reading of Disneyland to propose a reading of the whole of the United States as a postmodern fantasy (see **Postmodernism**).

In the spirit of our exhorting you to read key writers in their own words rather than through the filter of a critic or commentator (who will often have an ideological axe to grind) we recommend you read extract 71, which is excerpted from Edward Said's groundbreaking book *Orientalism* (see **Postcolonialism**).

To get hold of the previous two texts all you need to do is visit your school, college or public library or a bookstore with a reasonable range of academic textbooks. We can't tell you what section title to look under because different bookstores use different classifications. Even different branches of Waterstones use different names for the same selections of books. We found copies of *Beginning Theory* and *Communication Studies: The Essential Resource* in the Sociology & Cultural Studies section of a local Waterstones bookstore. To access the third resource we're recommending you need to go to:

http://www.aber.ac.uk/media/index.html

and that will get you to the main Directory of:

THE MEDIA AND COMMUNICATIONS STUDIES (MCS) SITE OF THE UNIVERSITY OF WALES AT ABERYSTWITH WEBSITE

where you will see the list of the fifteen areas into which the website is divided.

(At this point we should issue a warning. We can't give you a definitive guide to the website because it's alive, changing, expanding; unlike a book it's not fixed. First established by Daniel Chandler in 1995, the website now describes itself as 'a "meta-index" to Internet-based resources useful in the academic study of media and communication' where any number of writers now post essays.)

The fifteen areas are:

Active Interpretation	Advertising	Film Studies
Gender, Ethnicity	General Issues	General Reference
IT and Telecoms	Media Education	Media Influence
News Media	Pop Music/Youth	Textual Analysis
TV and Radio	Visual Image	Written Spoken

Click on any of these fifteen areas and you'll access its own Directory. All fifteen areas have postings that will make useful reading for students of Communication Studies, so explore the website at your leisure. But we'd like to recommend three areas that are particularly useful for beginners.

Click on Textual Analysis and you'll go to its own Directory. There are eight headings here: Content Analysis; Ideological Analysis; Rhetorical Analysis; Discourse Analysis (see **Dis-**

course **Analysis**); Intertextuality; Semiotics (see **Semiotics**); Genre Theory; and Narratology.

Click on Semiotics and you'll be presented with a list (arranged alphabetically by authors' family names) of essays about semiotics which can be accessed by clicking on the link on the website. This Directory also records how many times each link has been accessed that week. We would particularly recommend you read three of Daniel Chandler's essays on semiotics: 'Semiotics: The Basics' (2001), Semiotics for Beginners' (1995) and 'Semiotic Analysis of Advertisements' (1997).

Click on General Issues and you'll go to its Directory. There you'll you find ten areas, four of which we especially recommend: Communication and Media Theory (see **What is Communication Studies?**); Non-Verbal Communication (see **Non-Verbal Communication**); History of Communication and Media (see **Communication Studies in the UK**); and Research into Media/Communication (see **Which Theory for Communication Studies?**).

Click on Gender, Ethnicity and you'll go to its own Directory. There are six headings here: Ethnicity; Representation (see **Mass Communication**); Gender (see **Gender Criticism**); Social and Personal Identity (see **From Intrapersonal Communication to Interpersonal Communication to Group Communication**); Queer Theory (see **Gender Criticism**); and Social Class (see **Historical Materialism**).

As we indicated at the beginning of this introduction to the MCS website, it has expanded considerably since it was first established in 1995. The parts of the site we have recommended here are most useful for students starting out in Communication Studies. But don't forget MCS – bookmark it on your PC. As you progress in your studies we can't believe you won't need to go back to the site as it features links to work by many eminent scholars of and commentators on Communication and Media Studies.

PART II
STUDY SKILLS IN COMMUNICATION STUDIES

PART I

7 BECOMING AN EFFECTIVE COMMUNICATION STUDIES STUDENT

You will most likely have been introduced to study skills when you were at school or college. In what follows we don't intend to presume you know nothing at all about how to prepare yourself for and organise yourself in your undergraduate work in Communication Studies. Rather, what we will do is to contextualise what you already know and can do within a UK higher education context where there is increasing emphasis on independent study.

You will notice a big difference between studying at school, sixth form college or further education college and at university. You will be expected to take much more responsibility for your own learning. Whereas before the emphasis was on your responding to the requirements and demands of your teachers, you will now find that you need to take the initiative more and need to become an independent learner. Typically you might find that your course has around ten hours of actual 'contact time' each week – that is, actual timetabled classes. If all that you do is attend these, you will not develop a good grasp of your subject. Most courses provide reading lists, often including specific texts to be read before particular lectures or seminars. It is important to read this material carefully, before and after the class, if you want to get to grips with the material. The reading lists will usually contain Essential Reading, which you must study in order to understand the course fully, and Suggested Reading, from which you are expected to select material that particularly interests you, in order to broaden your understanding and make it your own. Most of the items on such lists, whether books or research papers, will have bibliographies which enable you to personalise your approach to the topic studied further.

The fact that you have only a few hours of scheduled classes each week does not mean that you are left entirely to your own devices for the rest of your learning. It is important that you should see and use your lecturers, as well as librarians, technicians, administrative staff and other people as resources on whom you can call. Most universities have a system of personal tutors whose job it is to provide support for a small number of students. This may include 'pastoral' support for students with personal, family, money or health problems as well as advice and assistance with students' learning. To get the best out of this system, you need to be proactive and take the initiative, but you also need to show that you are making the effort to learn. If you go to a tutor having read a couple of items from the reading list and asking for advice on how to find out more about one or more of the topics they cover, she will be able to give you a lot more help than if you simply turn up with questions you could have answered for yourself by doing the reading. If you ask a question which could be answered by consulting something the lecturer has already made available to you (through print or e-learning materials), you will make a poor impression.

Even in the age of digital information, indeed especially in that age, university libraries are a major resource for your learning. In addition to books and journals, of course, they contain a range of material that you can consult.

Books are no longer the only contents of a library; that's why many libraries are now being renamed 'information resource centres'. But books are still important (obviously so – if we didn't think this, we wouldn't have written this one). Many course tutors will advise you that one or two titles are essential or recommended purchases, but unless you are very rich, you are unlikely to be able to buy and own anything like enough of the books you will need to consult in the course of your degree. Books are more portable than most electronic media. Unlike most electronic media (at least at the time of writing) books can be carried around and consulted at times when you would otherwise be doing nothing – on buses and trains, while waiting for classes, while eating or waiting for friends in a café or bar. If you cultivate the habit of reading almost wherever you are (and not limiting yourself to reading only in specially designated 'reading' locations) you will be surprised how much you can learn quite easily in a few minutes at a time. Indeed, many learning theorists argue that learning undertaken in short, frequent sessions is more effect-ive than learning undertaken in long continuous sessions. That's why, if you are attempting to read to understand and to remember, you shouldn't try to do this for more than 50 minutes in any 60-minute time-frame.

The other traditional printed resources in libraries are journals. These range from the popular newspapers and magazines with which you will be familiar and which will provide some of the material for you to study this subject to the rather more studious, peer-reviewed academic research journals. These latter often look rather austere and off-putting to students (and to anyone else, come to that) but it is a good idea to get into the habit of looking at them early in your undergraduate career. Much of the material may seem rather dry at first but if you skim through them you will eventually find something that sparks your interest. There are two good reasons for making the acquaintance of the journals early on in your course. The first is that they contain the latest ideas and studies in the field and so they are more up-to-the-minute than most textbooks. This means you can find out what is being studied now and what the latest opin-ions are. In Communication Studies, it is important to be up-to-date. The second reason is that if you glance regularly through the journals – no one suggests you should read them from cover to cover – you will begin to get the flavour of the academic styles of writing, ways of making references and the structures of papers that the discipline uses. If you use this as a model for your own written work, it will make you sound more authoritative and scholarly. The American poet Ezra Pound used to advise young poets to write pastiches of poems to become better poets. A pastiche is a new work in the recognisable writing style of another writer. It's probably not something we're conscious of, but when we start writing academically we tend to copy earlier writers' work or to incorporate elements of their writing style into our own. Because everyone has access to so much writing nowadays maybe all writing is a postmodern collection of previous writers' styles.

It's important that we pause for a moment here and think more about what it actually means to read. There are many false assumptions about reading, and about how we take in and absorb information from reading. Try timing yourself reading and work out how many words per minute (w.p.m.) you can get through. The result could prove startling either because of the slow speed at which you read or, if you try the exercise a few times, because you may find you have *only one* reading speed. Reading for the efficient taking in of information is a skill that *has* to be learned. For one thing you could be spending much more time than is necessary, taking up a lot of your precious time, by virtue of reading inefficiently. It's often thought that the faster you read the less you take in, but the opposite is often true. In other words, if you read slowly you can very easily get bored and drift away. When your attention wanders it's easy to think you're reading something but in fact you're only looking at it, staring at it and are taking in nothing at all. The faster you read the quicker you get through something, the less time you take up, and the less risk you run of getting tired and bored. Just as a car has different gears and can travel at different speeds, which all have their uses in different situations, so you should have different speeds for reading different kinds of texts because your purpose in reading them will not always be the same. If you always read at the same speed you're likely to waste an awful lot of time and miss out on an awful lot of information.

Here's an explanation about five different types of reading speed and five different types of reading. Reading is as much a part of your Communication Studies Toolkit as the critical perspectives we looked at in Chapter 5. Do your best to develop and extend the range of reading speeds with which you can tackle texts in your studies.

Studying: reading speed – 5/10–200 w.p.m.

If you've been directed to do some close reading of a text or if you need to read something carefully for your own researches this will require you giving special attention to detail, to consider the meanings and the implications of what you're reading, to go back over the text (once or twice or more!), and to make notes on what you've read. This is not reading slowly for the sake of it but reading at what averages out as a slow speed because you were endeavouring to ensure you had fully grasped the text's meanings and implications.

Slow reading: reading speed – 150–300 w.p.m.

This is either the standard reading speed of the slow and inefficient reader or it's the speed of the efficient reader coping with a difficult text that contains ideas, concepts, words or phrases that they haven't met before. Having to use a dictionary or to cross-check with other texts or to visit a bookmarked website can all work together to create this slow average speed. It is perfectly appropriate to read at this speed if you are coping with difficult material; it is not appropriate to read at this speed as a matter of course, for simple everyday texts.

Rapid reading: reading speed – 300–800 w.p.m.

For most general texts, things you're familiar with (both in terms of content and form) you should easily achieve and maintain a reading speed in this range. If you read at a speed of less then 300 w.p.m. for everyday reading then you're wasting your time. If you think that your slow reading is a way of taking in everything think about this: for everyday purposes it's not necessary to exceed a level of about 70 per cent comprehension and retention of a text's contents. Indeed, it's often the case that there isn't more than 70 per cent of the text that actually needs to be attended to and remembered. When people speak they wrap up what they're saying with more words than are necessary (through, for example, repetition and emphasis) so too when people write they wrap up or pad out what they're saying with more words than are necessary. There will be irrelevant material in many texts that are read rapidly.

Skimming: reading speed – 800–1,000 w.p.m.

If you have a clear and precise idea of what you are looking for when you are reading something, you don't need to read every single word or phrase in the text you have before you. Quickly moving your eyes from left to right and from the top of the page to the bottom you'll find that – with practice – you can locate the precise information you're looking for. Obviously, if the text is clearly laid out it means that it can be easily skimmed. (It's worth bearing this in mind if you are considering a career as a professional communicator for the speed at which someone reads a text is often dictated by the way in which the text has not only been written but also how it has been presented.) As a skill, skimming is most useful when you are examining material to grasp the gist or general meaning of a text which is a preliminary stage in research for an in-depth or extended piece of work.

Scanning: reading speed – 1,000–2,000 w.p.m.

If you've managed to skim over material you can take it that bit further and increase your speed until you are actually scanning texts. This is a useful skill to develop when examining pages of journals, reference documents, cards in a file or indexes of books. What you are seeking when scanning is a really precise piece of information – a statistic, a key phrase in a famous quotation from a leading figure in Communication Studies, a date, a percentage, a page reference. It will take a lot of practice to get up to these speeds but when you achieve them you will find that you save yourself a lot of time and trouble. You can achieve seemingly impossible speeds. Practise sufficiently and you'll find that what you're looking for positively leaps off the page at you!

Used appropriately, books and journals will often lead you to more serendipitous learning and happier coincidences than electronic media. We have generally found that this makes learning more enjoyable and interesting and that, in turn, makes it easier, so we don't think you should give up on paper-based information just yet. Of course, there are lots more types of sources.

Before considering these, here is a final tip about written sources. Many students get by in their work by quoting what are called secondary sources. This means books, such as textbooks, that describe or refer to the work of other researchers. Thus, in writing an essay on psychoanalysis, many students will confine their reading to a few of the books that refer to it, perhaps alongside some material on Freud from a web-page. You will get much more out of your studies by looking at the original sources, in this case, for example, Freud's book *The Psychopathology of Everyday Life* (see **Further Reading**). Sometimes you will find this material (what is termed a primary source) difficult, but often, as in Freud's case, you will be pleasantly surprised; Freud is in fact a clearer and easier writer than many of the people who have written about him! Reading primary sources will give you a greater sense of what the original source is all about. And quoting from primary sources in your submitted assignments will give them more authority.

There is another problem or danger with secondary sources; this is the fact that many of them could be classified more properly as tertiary sources. In other words, writers of some introductory or explanatory texts do not go to the primary sources, the original texts, but rather go to secondary texts. Thus the original works, the original words, have been doubly diluted in the process of writing this new book. Maybe that's why Marx himself, when confronted with supposedly Marxist writing, declared that if this was Marxism then he was no Marxist. In the first – not the last – place read de Beauvoir, read Foucault, read Freud, read Marx, read Mulvey, read Said.

Besides these more traditional types of printed resource the library will contain a range of audiovisual material, usually including prints and slides, video and audio recordings, both off-air (that is, recorded as they were broadcast) and purpose-recorded (for example, video recording of lectures by leading academics). The more different sorts of resource you use the deeper will be the understanding you develop. This is because we process different types of information using different parts of the brain and the more of your brain you use in studying a subject the wider and deeper your knowledge of it will be. So use a range of different sources when looking up a topic.

The other main type of resource to be found in the library is electronic information. University libraries give you access to a huge amount of information stored on databases, the contents of other libraries, archives and electronic publications. Of course, some of these are publicly available via the Internet but there are many more specialised and detailed ones available on subscription to libraries. Many of these are of especial interest to Communication Studies students, such as the ProQuest database of newspaper articles.

The Internet is a good source of basic information. These days it seems hard to believe that we managed without it even fifteen years ago, but it has dangers as well as advantages for students. The World Wide Web is a rich storehouse of all kinds of information, but it is completely unregulated. Put bluntly, any fool can publish his opinions or her version of the facts on the Net. It is no more reliable a source in itself than gossip or graffiti (both of which, of course, have their place). Thus you need to be much more cautious about information from the Net than from printed sources. Of course, there are some wrong, silly and stupid things in print as well, but the fact that someone has paid to print, publish and distribute them indicates at least that they are not the ravings of one deranged individual, unless that individual is a respected academic.

Just as some publishers' imprints will indicate more academic credibility than others, so some websites, such as those operated by universities, research institutes and government bodies, can be considered more reliable than others. You need to think carefully about how reputable a source is before you make use of it.

Whatever type of resource you are consulting it is very important that you should take notes. It is very easy to read a paper, watch a video or access a website, think you understand it and then find out the next day that you don't remember much, if anything, that you learned from it. Taking notes as you are reading or watching means you will have a record to jog your memory. Just as important, even if you never look at the notes again, the simple act of taking them will aid your memory because you are actively processing the information rather than merely passively observing it. Some people like to take notes on A4 pads so they can file them in an orderly way in ring binders. Others prefer to keep a pocket notebook with them at all times so they can always make notes. The A4 method leads to tidier records but is bulky. The pocket book will always be with you, but the information, unless you spend a lot of time regularly indexing it, will be harder to track down. What works for you is something you can best find out by experiment. There is no one superior system. What is vital is that you have a system (see **Notes in Lectures**).

Keeping notes is something you should be doing at other times, too. When you read something relevant to your course in a newspaper or see it on television or hear it on the radio make a note and remember to write down where it came from. You never know when something will give you a fresh insight into your studies and this is probably more true in areas of study such as Communication, Media or Cultural Studies than most disciplines. (Perhaps Sociology comes close.) The objects of Communication Studies are frequently ripped from the day's newspaper headlines or the afternoon's broadcast television. What might appear to be at the margins of society may be central to the study of Communication.

Most Communication Studies courses are largely, if not entirely, continually assessed by regular assignments. If students have a choice of assignment titles it can be tempting (especially under the time-pressure forced on many students today by the need to do paid work to support the cost of their studies) to study only those parts of the course or module that relate to the assignments they are going to do. While this can sometimes be a legitimate strategy in times of real emergency, we strongly warn you against making it your general approach. On the contrary, you should try to ensure that you study all aspects of the course and feel that you have an overall command of the subject in its entirety. In the end this will make your learning easier since, as you go on through your years of study at university, you will build on the earlier knowledge and gain the confidence that comes from acquiring a broad understanding of your discipline. This will make the more advanced material you study in your second and third years much easier to understand. Of course, it would not make sense to try to know everything about everything. You should undertake the basic reading on each topic but go into depth in those areas that particularly interest you. It is in these areas that you will get the most out of your studies if you regard your tutors and librarians as sources of advice.

One of the consequences of moving from a form of education where the teacher's job is to instil a body of information in the students to one in which you take more responsibility for your own learning is that you will learn much more if you participate in discussion. Most courses and modules will include a significant amount of time in which you are invited to engage in a discussion of the material from a reading or a lecture with one or more tutors and other students. Lots of people find this quite intimidating. This is a shame because it is one of the best ways to learn about any subject. There are two reasons why many people don't get anything like as much out of these sessions (which are usually called seminars or tutorials). One is that they didn't read the material or pay attention in the lecture. Here, obviously, the cure for this problem is in your hands. The other is shyness. Most of us find it difficult to be the first one to speak up, especially if we are in a group of people we don't know very well. Some tutors are better than others at coaxing students to get started in discussion and some students are more confident than others. However, there is something everyone can do to help overcome shyness and take a full part. Like any form of public speaking, the key to confidence is preparation. Before you go into the seminar, look through the reading, or lecture notes, if that's what it will be based on, and write down two or three things that you particularly thought interesting or difficult about it. When asked to say something, you will then be ready to say either 'I thought it was interesting that . . .' or 'I didn't quite understand this part. Could you explain it?' If everybody undertakes this elementary preparation, which need only take a few seconds, the seminar will be much more successful and all participants (students and teachers alike) will get much more out of it.

Today's universities, particularly the modern universities in which most Communication Studies departments are to be found, are finding it increasingly difficult to provide as much of this sort of teaching as they would like because student numbers are rising faster than staff numbers as a result of various decisions by central government. This is a shame because discussion and debate are a large part of the traditional university experience and a very valuable way to learn. You should therefore look out for opportunities to engage in such activities outside of your timetabled classes. Keep an eye on noticeboards – material or electronic – for information about visiting speakers, guest lectures, research seminars, and so on. Often undergraduate students feel that these activities are not meant for them, but they are usually open to everyone and, in the experience of the writers of this book, everyone has always been made welcome at them. Don't be afraid to go along. All students are members of the university and encouraged to take part in its scholarly activities, even if they've only been there a few weeks!

8 TIME MANAGEMENT

There are many things you can do to make yourself a more effective student in terms of:

Motivation	Why am I studying Communication?
Gratification	How do I keep myself studying Communication?
Climate	How do I maintain my attention when studying?
Location	Where should I study Communication?
Active study	How do I go about making my study of Communication active and not passive?
Study techniques	What techniques or strategies should I adopt when studying Communication?

It's vital that you have satisfactory answers to all of these questions before you commit to actual study, particularly when you consider that much of the structures in which you've previously studied have been built for you by your teachers. You are now going to be an independent learner and you will have to generate the resources to start, continue and complete work from within yourself. None of your resources will be worth anything if you can't manage your time effectively.

Given that you are human like the rest of us you will have all kinds of needs and likes that you are used to meeting or enjoying in any given week. In addition, you will have countless matters pressing on your mind apart from your studies of Communication. The problem is how to ensure that your meeting of your needs, your enjoyment of your likes and your dwelling on pressing matters do not intrude on your study time. The answer is to acknowledge that all of these things exist, to note them down and to timetable them away. The preparation of weekly timetables in which all of these items are factored in can help.

For study purposes we advise you build every aspect of your life in any given week at university into your personal timetable. Include such items as travel, work, eating, sleeping, leisure, recreation and love. When you first attempt this you might find you end up with a 17-hour day (because you have no sound grasp of everything you do in any given day) or a 29-hour day (because you have an inflated idea of what you do each day or because you cannot accurately time-cost your regular days).

Before you sit down to make your first attempt at doing this exercise you will have a vague, ill-formed and ill-defined notion of the week ahead. You will be vaguely aware that you have some Communication Research work to do; that you intend to go to the union bar on two nights; that you have to travel to and from university; that you have some reading to do; that you want to listen to some new CDs you bought last weekend; that you need to watch a DVD of *House of Games* (if you can find it; you were recommended to watch it in something you read somewhere but it seems a really old film); that you promised yourself you would go to the gym twice this week; and that you have some serious clothes shopping to do.

Once you have committed to organising all aspects of your life into a timetable, a more reasonable and more ordered view of the week ahead will emerge.

The important feature of this approach to timetabling your life is that you have included everything. Many study plans fail because students are not sufficiently honest about all the things they do in a week: they are either pretending to themselves that they are a more diligent student than they actually are, or they simply don't have an accurate overview of all that they do in any given week.

The timetable will reflect all kinds of aspects of your life because it factors them all in.

If you have certain needs that have to be met or things you enjoy doing, timetable these into your week. If your love life is worth enjoying or if you have specific television programmes you want to see, allocate specific times at which you will watch them. Don't try to do two things at once. Do one thing at a time and enjoy each individual activity to the full. In this way you will achieve life, social and study goals.

With pressing matters timetable them away and deal with them at a time and in a place that is appropriate. The timetabling away of pressing matters will not make them go away; what it will do is to ensure that they do not intrude on your study time and that they are dealt with at the appropriate time and in the appropriate place. Harsh as it may seem, these are irrelevant and intrusive stimuli and as such need to be removed.

Finally, remove any people who might intrude on your study time. At home, at work and in your social circle inform family, colleagues and friends politely but firmly that you have studies to complete and that you cannot afford to be disturbed. Any family or set of friends worth having will realise that you want to make a success of your Communication Studies course and that if they interfere with your studies, then they will get the worst of you in their contact with you.

9   USING A TUTORIAL

A tutorial is a meeting between one or more tutors and one or more students to discuss the student's work. A tutorial is distinct from a seminar, which is about group discussion and is generally linked to a particular lecture or set of readings. Terminologies vary between institutions, but generally a tutorial is a meeting of one lecturer and one student.

Just as terminologies vary from university to university, so too do universities vary in the way they organise academic and pastoral support for students. Some have a system of personal tutors who are allocated to the student when she starts her course and who remain her tutor for the duration of her programme of study. Others provide this level of support through a system of year tutors. Still others will advise students to seek academic help from the designated module or course tutor. You should make sure that you find out during your induction ('freshers' week') who you can go to if you need help, either with your work or with other problems.

Tutorials may be scheduled as part of your timetabled classes, but the changing ratio of students to teaching staff in UK universities often makes this a prohibitively expensive form of teaching. Tutorials are more likely to take place as an ad hoc arrangement between a student and a tutor to address a specific issue or problem.

Sometimes the tutorial is initiated by the tutor. This is most likely to happen at the start of the student's course in order to get to know each other and to reassure the student that support is available. Tutors may also invite students to tutorials if they feel that the student has misunderstood some point of the course, for example in an assignment.

More often, a student requests a tutorial with a tutor to clarify or explain some aspect of their learning. Tutors will normally seek to give a clear explanation of the points at issue and may recommend additional reading or viewing to help the student understanding. Students may also seek advice from tutors in this way about free choice or option modules, about work placements, or other aspects of the course.

Some universities' teaching staff publish timetables detailing their availability to offer tutorials. These take the form of a few hours a week, on different days where students may sign themselves in at, say 10–15-minute intervals for brief tutorials relating to ongoing coursework.

The key to getting the most out of tutorials, like so much in life, is preparation. Before you go to see your tutor make sure you are clear what it is you need to know. If you are asking for clarification of part of the lecturer's teaching, make sure you have read the notes you took in the lecture, that you have read the associated texts and that you have written down which parts you don't understand and, if possible, why. Lecturers have a lot of demands on their time in addition to their undergraduate teaching and, while they will normally be very happy to take the time to explain points you are finding difficult, they will be less able to help you if you have not done your share of the learning process. It is not always a good idea to miss a lecture without good reason, to ignore the associated reading and then to go to the lecturer and ask them what the lecture was all about. That said, if you have missed one or more classes, you should make an effort to catch up as quickly as you can. Don't leave it until the day before the submission of the coursework assignment or the sitting of the examination! Get copies of any handouts or readings that were given out, ask a friend if you can make a photocopy of their notes, see how much sense you can make of the material, and then go to your tutor to check you've got it right.

The other form of tutorial you will probably experience is associated with group project work. This is an integral part of much university work these days and nowhere more so than in Communication Studies. On all such courses of which the present authors are aware group work forms a part not only of the learning process but also of the assessment regime.

Groups will normally be allocated a tutor and will be expected to meet with her on a number of occasions to discuss the progress of the project. They will meet to discuss the initial idea, they will meet to discuss the written brief, they will meet as the tutor progress-chases them, they will meet to discuss the completed project, and they will meet to facilitate the process of self-evaluation. The tutor will seek to ensure that the group has a clear understanding of the project, that it draws up a viable plan and that it carries it out. Normally, this will involve the allocation of specific tasks and roles to the group members.

Finally, a student may seek tutorial support because he has personal problems apart from his actual learning. These might be to do with health, stress, money, family, relationships and a range of other difficulties. Tutors are not experts in solving all these problems, although if they have been doing the job for some time, they are likely to be able to reassure you that previous cases of a similar type have turned up in the past and have been satisfactorily resolved. It is very easy to feel isolated as a student, often away from home for the first time and surrounded by strangers, and yet students in reality are able to access a wide range of support services such as health professionals, counsellors, religious advisers, financial advisers, legal experts, and so on, usually free of charge. While your tutor will not be an expert in all these fields she will know where and how to refer you for professional advice and support.

To understand better how tutorials can work for students and teachers alike we now present you with some case studies, all set in a fictional but we hope not too fictional setting.

Jaz and Daniel are both students in the first year of the BA in Communication Studies at Barchester Metropolitan University. Like all first year students they find that, from time to time, things don't go smoothly and they need to think carefully about what they're doing and sometimes to seek help from tutors or fellow students.

Luckily they each, in their different ways, are sensible enough not to panic or give up, and in this way they find solutions to their difficulties. As a result their tutors expect them both to pass the first year and progress successfully – now on their way to achieving good honours degrees.

Case Study – 1 Jaz doesn't understand the lecture

Jaz has been attending classes and taking notes regularly (except for the day after her flatmate's birthday party) and thought she was understanding everything just fine. Now, however, the first assignment is due next week and she is having a crisis of confidence. She thought she understood the concepts of first- and second-order signification when they had the lecture and even took part in the seminar discussion, but now she tries to explain it to herself she's not certain any more. Looking back over the notes from the previous weeks she begins to wonder if she's really got it right about paradigms and syntagms as well. Luckily she remembers that the first thing her tutor told her was what to do in these circumstances and she decides to take her advice.

Jaz gets out all the notes and handouts for the module so far and goes through them in order. When she comes to something she's not sure of, she makes a note. Armed with these notes she makes an appointment to see Jane, her tutor. At the tutorial, Jaz asks for clarification about the orders of signification and Jane explains that first-order signification ('denotation') is the literal meaning of a text whereas second-order signification ('connotation') is about the associations the reader has with that meaning. They discuss how they apply to a short sequence from a soap episode they both watched last night and that makes the concepts clearer.

After leaving the tutorial, Jaz is angry with herself because she forgot to ask Jane about paradigms and syntagms. Rather than book another appointment she sends Jane an email and gets a reply calling her attention to a part of the website they have talked about where the concepts of paradigms and syntagms are explained. Jane offers Jaz another tutorial time but once she's read the tutorial she is happy that she did understand it properly and so she doesn't need to take up the offer.

Case Study 2 – Daniel needs help with his essay

Daniel is coming to the end of his first year and has to write an essay on gender criticism. Although he went to the lectures, to be honest, he didn't find this part of the course very interesting and now he is beginning to wish he had paid more attention. He goes to see his tutor and asks what he should do.

At first, Paul, his tutor is a little irritated with Daniel who has come unprepared and seems to have made little effort to address the problem himself. Paul points out that his job is to teach him, not to write his essays for him, but Daniel realises that he needs to take more responsibility for his own learning and says so. Then he asks Paul's advice how he should proceed.

Paul takes Daniel through the stages of writing an essay: clarifying the title and what it is asking for (translating the essay's title), initial reading and notes, brainstorming ideas, putting them into a logical order, using supporting reading to back up the argument, and structuring it with an introduction and a conclusion (the bookends to the body of the essay).

Then they talk about the subject of the essay. To his surprise, Daniel realises that he does remember more of the lecture than he had thought as they talk about it. They sketch a very general essay plan and Paul suggests some further reading.

Daniel asks Paul about the reference system he should use and Paul shows him the pages on the university's computerised learning support system that has pages devoted to the convention of referencing within academic essays.

10 NOTES IN LECTURES

Before we consider how to go about effective note-taking in lectures we need to look at some aspects of what we would term the physiology of learning. In other words, let's look at some of the ways in which we function as human beings and be aware of this when we are studying in general, and when we are attending lectures specifically.

In any given lecture's sixty-minute time-frame a pattern is clearly discernible in terms of what are called attention levels and retention levels. Our attention levels are simply the extent to which we are awake and receptive to the ideas being presented to us by our teachers. Our retention levels are the percentage of information we retain and can recall from our teachers' lectures. At the beginning of the one-hour lecture students will be alert and receptive, and will retain a large amount of information offered them by their Communication Studies lecturer. They might even take accurate, full notes. Gradually, the students' receptivity levels decline and for the middle twenty minutes very little information is retained. Only if something out of the ordinary happens will the students remember it: the teacher might offer a striking image or a memorable example. (These are the things that students often remember years after they've stopped being students.) Shortly after this incident the students will pay close attention to the lecturer on the chance that another striking image or memorable example will be offered; but it isn't and so the students turn off again. For these middle twenty minutes the lecturer's voice often barely affects students, existing only as a vague drone in the background. But once the half-way and then the two-thirds marks are passed things begin to pick up. Instead of mentally ticking off the minutes that have gone students begin to count how many minutes are left to go. This signals a return to an active rather than a passive role and as a result of this the students are more alert and retain quite a lot of information on offer – never as much as the first twenty minutes, but immeasurably more than in the middle twenty minutes.

Of course, an astute lecturer who is aware of this pattern could well organise the hour's lecture to accommodate these falling and rising levels of attention and retention. Thus she could plan the lecture as follows:

Phase 1 (0–20 minutes)

'What I want to do is . . . '

Make main points – A B C

Break up main points into sub-headings

Aa Bb Cc

Phase 2 (21–40 minutes)

'Did I ever tell you?'

Offer examples that illustrate main points and subsidiary points

Phase 3 (41–60 minutes)

'The point of all this has been . . . '

Tie loose ends together

Recap main points – A B C

This might appear to waste time but a professional communicator should be careful not to overtax their audience. It's physically impossible for students to take full, detailed and accurate notes for every minute of a one-hour lecture. It's difficult to listen and take notes at the same time, so if two really important points are made one after the other it's likely that students will miss the second one. The professional communicator should allow their audience time to put down their pens to allow them to just listen rather than having to scribble madly all the time. An example offered might just clarify a point and information can be absorbed when one is relaxing. If both the lecturer and the students are aware of this pattern then it's possible for the lecturer to direct the lecture almost like a theatre director or orchestra conductor and give the students cues or signals as to what they should do and when they should do it. Thus a lecturer might well use phrases such as:

'The point I'm making here is . . .'

'What this means is . . .'

'This isn't always the case. An exception is . . .'

'What you should note here is . . .'

Efficient listeners will pick up on these key phrases or cues and realise that information is on the way, pick up their pens and make a note of it.

The key to all effective study is to make it as active as you possibly can. Here's some advice for effective note-taking in lectures. The advice relates not only to how you can take effective notes during lectures, but to how you can consolidate those notes after the lecture's over.

Divide your file paper in half by drawing a line from top to bottom. Use the left-hand side of the page only. Leave the right-hand side blank for the time being.

When listening to a lecture always note the speaker and the topic. This helps you build up a referencing system and enables you to have quick and easy access to your notes: you don't want to have to read all of your notes to find out what the topic was.

Listen to the lecture and note down key words, phrases and ideas. Never attempt to take down exactly what is said; that's something that only people with shorthand can do. If you don't manage to take a note of something said, leave a gap. Once the lecturer's finished delivering their lecture chase up someone who got the point and fill in the empty space.

Learn to follow the gist (the general meaning) of what's being said. Much of what lecturers say is mere mannerism and has no meaning: but, um, ah, however, as it were, personally speaking, we can thus see, for myself, let us consider.

When the lecturer has finished and your notes are completed go back to the beginning as soon as possible and begin reading over your notes. On the right-hand side of the page note down the points you have missed (maybe the connection from one point to another isn't clear), your own comments, criticisms and ideas. Indicate the especially important points that you wish to remember and those points you want to follow up. It's useful to develop a personal coding system here where you can see for yourself with a brief symbol how important a point is.

Then combine both the left-hand and the right-hand side of your file paper to produce a summary of the lecture.

If you work in this way not only will you end up with effective summaries of lectures but you will also have been engaged in an active learning exercise. By virtue of having written your notes, having read them while thinking and writing (a key factor in active learning), and by having combined the two sets of notes into one set of summary notes, you will have reinforced your own learning. Active learning means you will remember what you wrote. Sadly, many students take quite detailed notes in lectures but do not engage in the consolidation exercise of querying, combining and summary writing. This means they often don't look at their notes from the time of the lecture to the time of the examination; when they later consult their notes they often find them quite meaningless because the information was never consolidated or reinforced.

Active learning means you remembering what you wrote. It makes the time you spent working on your notes well worth it, because your notes will speak to you and will trigger all kinds of memories of the time you were in the lecture or were working on your notes.

11 WRITING SKILLS

Crunch-time for most students is when they have to actually write an essay. It's all very well agonising or joking about essays with friends in social situations, but eventually all students have to confront sheets of blank paper or blank PC monitors and begin writing their essays. A major hurdle for many students is the very first essay they write at university. So we're going to follow another student through the many stages of the production of her first Communication Studies essay.

Case Study 3 – Laura writes her first Contemporary Critical Theory essay

Laura is another first year student of the BA in Communication Studies at Barchester Metropolitan University. This is the story of how she tackles one of her first pieces of written coursework for one of her first year modules.

Laura has taken the optional module in Contemporary Critical Theory, because she enjoyed English Literature at school and thought this would be quite similar. A lot of the approaches are, in fact, very close or identical to those used in literary criticism (see **Introduction** and **Further Reading**) and she has been interested to see how they can be applied to texts traditionally considered non-literary, such as television programmes, newspaper articles and popular songs. The assignment for this module is an essay of not more than 2,000 words. A choice of titles is offered. The assignment brief reads:

Write an essay of not more than 2,000 words with ONE of the following titles:

1. What do you understand to be the principal characteristics of structuralist and post-structuralist approaches to the study of texts?

2. Jean Baudrillard famously asserted that 'the Gulf War did not take place'. What did he mean by this?

3. What is the function of the concept of genre in the discussion of texts?

4. Compare any contemporary text using arguments drawn from at least two of the following approaches: psychoanalysis, feminism, postfeminism, Queer Theory, postcolonialism.

Laura decides to do number 4, so now she needs to choose her text and decide which perspectives to draw on. Her first problem is that there is an almost infinite number of texts to choose from. She feels that it would have been better if the lecturer had just specified one text or at least offered a limited choice, but she has noticed that her university lecturers are much less prescriptive about matters like this than the teachers at her school were. Although sometimes she finds this approach rather disconcertingly unstructured, she also recognises that it offers her a sense of freedom.

Laura likes films and is a big fan of science fiction so she thinks she might write the essay about a sci-fi movie, probably *The Matrix*, which is her favourite. Being a well-organised student, she sits down and makes a plan. First she turns to the section in her student handbook on essay technique. It tells her that the stages in essay writing are:

Essay title

Library notes

Free associating

Key points

Paragraph assembly/running order/structuring

Writing/scripting (recommend overwriting and editing rather than underwriting and stretching)

Editing

Polishing

Final structure

Bibliographies and referencing

Checking for spelling, grammar and syntax

She's got the title, so the next step is to visit the library. Actually she doesn't need to do this straight away because her room in the hall of residence has, like all student rooms, Internet access so she can consult the library catalogue and a number of databases online before going to the library to find the actual books that she needs. In fact, there is so much information about this film on the Web that she begins to think she may not need to use any books at all. However, she remembers being advised to use a range of sources so she decides she will look for references in books and journals as well.

Laura finds a large number of websites referring to *The Matrix* and quickly realises that one of the problems with using Web-based research is that they vary from very serious and scholarly sites to amateur, fan-based and downright silly ones. She wonders how she can be sure that the ones she uses will be appropriate for a university essay. Still, she saves the URL for a number of sites that interest her and then checks the library catalogue online and finds a review in a journal called *Sight and Sound* and two books on science fiction films.

After going to the library, borrowing the books and photocopying the review, Laura can start to make notes. Soon she has a couple of pages of them and is beginning to get an idea of how she will write the essay. The next step is to brainstorm ideas, so she takes a blank sheet of paper. She remembers what one of her Communication Studies tutors told her year group in one of their Study Skills sessions at the beginning of the first term of their first year: the technique of taking a piece of A4 lined paper and placing it on a worktop arranged in a landscape rather than a portrait fashion. The tutor explained that in this way students are less likely to be deceived by the formal linear pattern of the lines on the paper. They won't think that what is first written down on the piece of paper is the final running order of the completed piece of work in terms of the sequencing of ideas, points, examples and quotations. The tutor encouraged Laura's year group to write down everything they could think of in relation to the essay title first of all and not to try to assess whether points should or should not be included at this preliminary stage of writing the essay. The tutor advised her year group to leave her first ideas for a while and return to them later to begin the process of organising and shaping their material.

Laura quickly writes down all the ideas she can come up with about the film. She remembers the advice about leaving these initial ideas for a while and so she gives herself an evening off and goes to the cinema with her new friend, Jaz.

The next day she returns to the material and finds that she can very quickly put the ideas into an order that makes sense and leads to a defensible conclusion. Now she can begin to write. After four hours, she has written over 3,000 words and realises that she can't cover all the points she had planned to in a short essay. She decides what the key points for her argument are and discards the others. By the time she has written her conclusion she has nearly 3,500 words. It takes her the rest of the day to cut them down to 2,000 but, when she has, she feels that her essay reads well.

She goes through the essay, checking that she has a citation for each quotation or reference in it and constructs her bibliography. The system of referencing that she has been told to use is unfamiliar to her and, although she tries to follow the instructions in her course handbook, she isn't entirely confident she's got it right. Still, the deadline is coming up and she needs to take it to the Media Department office and hand it in and she does so reasonably confidently.

When she gets it back she finds she has got quite a good mark – 62 per cent – but realises she would have got more if she had remembered to run the spell check before printing off the final version. However, she is pleased that although she has made a couple of small mistakes in the bibliography, her tutor has commented favourably on the essay's construction. This makes her feel more confident about tackling essays in the future.

12 EXAMINATIONS: REVISING AND SITTING

For most students formal, time-constrained examinations are a great cause of anxiety. We can't teach you any techniques to alleviate any of the physical symptoms you might experience, but we can offer you lots of sound advice about how to tackle examinations.

Many Communication Studies course have moved to assessing students' work on a 100 per cent coursework basis. Even when they have examinations they are open book examinations. Some even offer students takeaway examinations where they are presented with examination question papers which are taken away for four weeks or so and then the completed examination essays or assignments are submitted. When you visit potential universities you might like to think about asking lecturing staff at open days or interview days about the assessment regime in the Communication Studies department. There are all sorts of reasons for being attracted to one particular university course and for many students that key question is whether or not there are examinations. If there are, what type of examinations are they?

In the advice that follows we are thinking about examinations in a very traditional sense: they are formal (that is, all students will sit at individual desks in a large space like a sports hall) and they will be time-constrained (that is, they will last two or three hours and an examination invigilator will announce when students can open their examination papers and start writing, and when they must stop writing and put down their pens).

The best preparation for successfully sitting examinations is to be an effective and conscientious student. Some students (very few in truth) are able to cram before taking an examination: they can sit down the night before an examination and read their notes and remember them with great clarity. But most students cannot do this and it does place a great strain on them, an unnecessary strain we would add. So if you have conscientiously attended all your lectures, seminars and tutorials; have undertaken the consolidation exercises we spoke about in **Notes in Lectures**; have researched, written and submitted all your coursework on time; and have taken care of yourself in terms of getting your life–work balance right (see **Time Management**), then you will actually be at the top of your game and will be at ease with yourself. You will be prepared for the examination because you will have all the information you need for writing your examination essays at your fingertips. This is the best kind of revision because it is active, ongoing and starts well before the night before the examination.

There are some other things you can do before you actually sit the examination.

You can review all the coursework you have submitted which has been marked and returned to you. Check to see if there are any habitual errors you make; check to see if you made any fundamental conceptual errors (have you really go a useful working definition of postmodernism for yourself?); check to see that you have key dates memorised (in, for example, the history of film).

You can look at past examination papers for the modules you are being tested on. All universities make hard copy of examinations available to students and most universities now have on-line archives of examination papers. (You could also speak with students in other years to ask them about their experiences.) Make sure you know what the format of the examination paper is so that you are not surprised by what you see when you open the paper in the examination room. Know how long the examination lasts. Know how many questions you will be asked to answer. Know if the examination paper will be divided up into sections where you will be expected to answer questions in all sections.

The night before you sit the examination don't try to engage in any lengthy, detailed revision. If your revision has been ongoing, then you will not need to do any swotting the night before. The best preparation you can do is to make sure you have a good night's sleep and that you are up bright and early on the day of the examination refreshed and ready for action. Do not, on any account, spend half the night poring over your notes, your files, your textbooks. There's an outside chance you might just learn something new (a very small chance), but you won't be alert enough to give of your best in the examination room.

On the day of the examination don't line up near the entrance to the examination room with stacks of files and folders under your arm desperately trying to cram in ideas at this very late stage. Even if you've transferred key ideas on to small file cards (about postcard size), don't try working through them. Making file cards is a sound revision method, but you should undertake this activity – both the making and the using – well before the day of the examination.

Make sure you have all the equipment you need for the examination: pens, pencils, erasers, rulers, whatever. Go into the examination room as soon as the invigilator invites you in. Get yourself seated at the desk you've been assigned to, have your ID card or examination card to hand, and DON'T PANIC!

When the start of the examination is signalled read through the question paper once – just to get an overall picture of the paper and the tasks to be undertaken. This reading will give you an overall understanding of what's being asked of you. Read through the paper a second time. This time make your reading more active by starting to underscore key words and phrases on the question paper. As you read through the paper this time start to sketch our your answers in rough.

If you are given a choice of questions to answer (say, three out of ten) don't make your decision as to which questions to answer immediately the examination starts. Try jotting down a few rough notes in response to all the questions. You might be surprised by the knowledge you have about certain questions. If you rule out certain questions immediately, you might make a poor decision. There might even be questions relating to a part of the module that you really didn't like or didn't get but about which you remember a lot. It could well be worth answering those questions.

Once you've decided which questions you are going to answer commit to a sequence or running order in which you will answer the questions. Rank the questions you're going to answer in order of the ease with which you think you'll answer them. If you rank three questions 1, 2 and 3, don't write the essays in this order. If you do you're likely to spend too much time on question 1 (and as it's your best answer you don't need to spend that much time on it) and not enough time on question 3 (when you'll be running out of time, energy and inspiration). Answer question 2 first: it's a strong question and you'll make a good job of it. Answer question 3 second: it's your worst question but if you tackle it when you are still alert and energetic, you will make a reasonable job of it. And answer question 1 last; it was always going to be your best answer and you could make a grand job of it in your sleep. (If you can come up with a better sequencing, all well and good. But you must have a game plan, you must know in what order you are going to tackle those questions; you mustn't leave anything to chance.)

Divide the time you have for the whole of the examination: if it's a three-hour examination and you've got to answer three questions we suggest you spend 55 minutes on each essay and use the remaining 15 minutes for essay plans and checking and revising.

Once you've written your examination answers go over them to check you've made the best job you can. Check for errors of fact. Check for gross errors in grammar, spelling or punctuation. Check to see you've actually answered the question that was asked of you. If you do spot something wrong simply strike a line through what you want to discount and write in the revised version. Don't try to scrub it out or to completely obliterate it. The examination paper marker might like to see what you thought was wrong (as you might have struck through a correct point and replaced it with an incorrect one).

When the invigilator announces the end of the examination there's nothing more you can do. That's it. Your fate is now in the hands of the markers.

After you've left the examination room don't engage in analysis of the paper. No amount of soul-searching will affect how the marker marks your examination paper. No amount of poring over the paper will get you any more marks. And don't get involved in lengthy discussions with fellow students about the paper: it'll only lead to feelings of, quite possibly, false hope or unfounded pessimism.

Be on top of your technique. Be mentally and physically alert when you sit examinations. When one examination is over get ready for the next one.

BIBLIOGRAPHY

Anderson, P. (1976) *Considerations on Western Marxism*, London: Verso.

Argyle, M. (1988) *Bodily Communication*, London: Methuen.

Austin, J. L. (1962) *How to Do Things with Words*, Oxford: Oxford University Press.

Barry, P. (2002) *Beginning Theory*, Manchester: Manchester University Press.

Barthes, R. (1977) *Image, Music, Text*, London: Fontana.

Barthes, R. (1993) *Mythologies*, London: Vintage.

de Beauvoir, S. (1988) *The Second Sex*, London: Penguin.

Beck, A., Bennett, P. and Wall, P. (2004) *Communication Studies: The Essential Resource*, London: Routledge.

Berger, J. (1972) *Ways of Seeing*, Harmondsworth: Penguin.

Britton, A. (1978/79) 'The Ideology of Screen', in *Movie* 26, 2–28.

Burr, V. (1999) *An Introduction to Social Constructionism*, London: Routledge.

Cherry, C. (1996) *On Human Communication*, Cambridge, MA: MIT Press.

Chomsky, N. and Herman, E. (1988) *Manufacturing Consent*, New York: Pantheon.

Cobley, P. (ed.) (1996) *The Communication Theory Reader*, London: Routledge.

Corner, J. (1998) *Studying Media*, Edinburgh: Edinburgh University Press.

Coulthard, M. (1985) *Introduction to Discourse Analysis*, London: Longman.

Culler, J. (1985) *Saussure*, London: Fontana.

Dixon, J. (1979) *Education 16–19: The Role of English and Communication*, London: Macmillan.

Eaglestone, R. (2000) *Doing English*, London: Routledge.

Eagleton, T. (1983) *Literary Theory: An Introduction*, Oxford: Blackwell.

Eco, U. (1981) *The Role of the Reader: Explorations in the Semiotics of Texts*, London: Hutchinson.

Finnegan, R. (2002) *Communicating: The Multiple Modes of Human Interconnection*, London: Routledge.

Fiske, J. (1990) *Introduction to Communication Studies*, London: Routledge.

Fortier, M. (1997) *Theory/Theatre*, London: Routledge.

Foucault, M. (1971) *Madness and Civilisation: a History of Insanity in the Age of Reason*, London: Routledge.

Foucault, M. (1980) *Power/Knowledge: Selected Interviews and Other Writings*, New York: Pantheon.

Foucault, M. (1991) *Discipline and Punish: the Birth of the Prison*, London: Penguin.

Foucault, M. (2003) The *Birth of the Clinic*, London: Routledge.

Freud, S. (1975) *The Psychopathology of Everyday Life*, London: Penguin.

Gergen, K. (1999) *Invitation to Social Construction*, London: Sage.

Greer, G. (2003) *The Female Eunuch*, London: Flamingo.

Guiraud, P. (1975) *Semiotics*, London: Routledge & Kegan Paul.

Hartley, P. (1997) *Group Communication*, London: Routledge.

Hartley, P. (1999) *Interpersonal Communication*, London: Routledge.

Hebdige, D. (1988) *Hiding in the Light*, London: Routledge.

Hedin, B. (2004) *Studio A: the Bob Dylan Reader*, New York: W. W. Norton & Co.

Jenks, C. (1989) *What is Postmodernism?*, London: Academy.

Kane, P. (1992) *Tinsel Show: Pop, Politics, Scotland*, Edinburgh: Polygon.

Katz, E. and Lazarsfeld, P. F. (1955) *Personal Influence: The Part Played by People in the Flow of Mass Communication*, London: Collier Macmillan.

Leader, D. and Groves, J. (1995) *Lacan for Beginners*, Trumpington: Icon.

Lechte, J. (1994) *Fifty Key Contemporary Thinkers*, London: Routledge.

Lyon, C. (ed.) (1986) *The International Dictionary of Films and Filmmakers, Volume 2: Directors*, London: Firethorn Press.

Lytotard, J.-F. (1984) *The Postmodern Condition*, Manchester: Manchester University Press.

McGarry, K. J. and Burrell, T. W. (1973) *Communication Studies*, London: Clive Bingley.

McLuhan, M. (2001) *Understanding Media: The Extension of Man*, London: Routledge.

Marx, K. and Engels, F. (1995) *Manifesto of the Communist Party*, New York: Signet Classics.

Menand, L. (2002) *The Metaphysical Club*, London: Flamingo.

Mills, S. (1996) *Discourse*, London: Routledge.

Morgan, J. and Welton, P. (1992) *See What I Mean?* London: Arnold.

Mulvey, L. (1992) *The Sexual Subject: A Screen Reader in Sexuality*, New York: Routledge.

Myers, K. (1986) *Understains*, London: Comedia.

Nunan, D. (1993) *Introducing Discourse Analysis*, London: Longman.

Olins, W. (2003) *On Brand*, London: Thames & Hudson.

Paglia, C. (1990) *Sexual Personae: Art and Decadence from Nefertiti to Emily Dickinson*, London: Yale University Press.

Paglia, C. (1993) *Vamps and Tramps*, London: Penguin.

Pease, A. (1984) *Body Language: How to Read Others' Thoughts by Their Gestures*, London: Sheldon Press.

Potter, J. and Wetherell, M. (1987) *Discourse and Social Psychology: Beyond Attitudes and Behaviour*, London: Sage.

Propp, V. (1958) *Morphology of the Folktale*, Austin, TX: University of Texas Press.

Said, E. (1994) *Orientalism*, New York: Vintage.

Saussure, F. de (1966) *Course in General Linguistics*, New York: McGraw-Hill.

Sedgwick, E. Kosofsky (1990) *The Epistemology of the Closet*, Berkeley: University of California Press.

Williamson, J. (1994) *Decoding Advertisements*, London: Marian Boyars.

Winchester, S. (2005) 'Nature's Way', *The Guardian* 4 January.

Winship, J. (1987) 'Handling sex', in R. Betterton (ed.) *Looking On*, London: Pandora.

Wolf, N. (1990) *The Beauty Myth: How Images of Beauty are Used against Women*, London: Vintage.

Wollstonecraft, M. (1792) *Vindication of the Rights of Woman: an Authoritative Text, Backgrounds, The Wollstonecraft Debate, Criticism / Mary Wollstonecraft*, ed. Carole H. Poston.

Wood, R. (1984) 'Jean-Luc Goddard', in C. Lyon (ed.) *The International Dictionary of Films and Filmmakers Volume 2 Directors/Filmmakers*, London: Firethorn.

Woolf, V. (1989) *A Room of One's Own*, New York: Harcourt.

X, M. (1992) *The Autobiography of Malcolm X/with the assistance of Alex Hayley*, New York: Ballantine.

INDEX